LIFE-SHOW

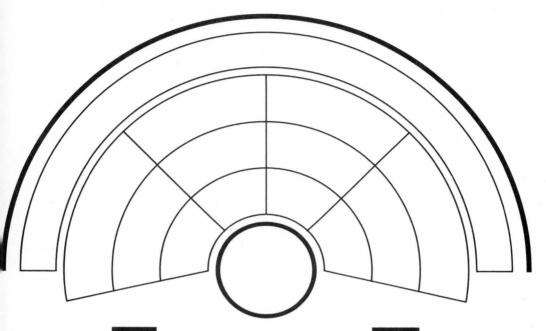

LIFE-SHOW

How to See Theater in Life and Life in Theater

John Lahr & Jonathan Price
Designed by Stephanie Tevonian
LIMELIGHT EDITIONS, NEW YORK

First Limelight Edition   October 1989
Copyright © 1973
by John Lahr and Jonathan Price

All rights reserved under international and Pan-American
Copyright Conventions. Published in the United States by
Proscenium Publishers Inc., New York and simultaneously in
Canada by Fitzhenry & Whiteside, Limited, Toronto.

Library of Congress Cataloging-in-Publication Data
Lahr, John, 1941–
Life-show : how to see theater in life and life in theater /
John Lahr & Jonathan Price.
p.   cm.
Reprint. Originally published: New York : Viking Press, 1973.
ISBN 0-87910-130-X : $12.95
1. Theater and society.   I. Price, Jonathan, 1941–
II. Title.
[PN2049.L3   1989]
792—dc20   89-12337
                                                CIP

Excerpts from *The Selling of the President 1968*
by Joe McGinniss, Copyright © 1969 by
Joemac Incorporated, are reprinted by
permission of Trident Press, a division of
Simon & Schuster, Inc.

ACKNOW-LEDGMENTS

Many people have contributed to the making of this book. The authors would like to thank them for their generosity and enthusiastic support: Gregory Armstrong, Richard Avedon, Georges and Ann Borchardt, Ann Hancock, Peter Kemeny, Anthea Lahr, Phoebe Larmore, Jane Toonkel.

CONTENTS

TO THE READER

This book is play. Discover its rules. Look at its boundaries. Imagine and make connections. You need nothing for the journey but eyes and an open mind.

Theater is a cultural mirror which reflects and distorts the reality of a time and a place.

We go to the theater to be entertained, but this is not a passive enjoyment. The audience filters the images and emotions from the stage and connects them with its own private world. The process of theater-going becomes a communal activity through which we can remember who we are and how we are, where we can touch the past and the present. The stage captures us from many angles, catching details we may have overlooked or refused to see: our costumes, our manners, our language, our "setting," our ideas.

When a play is prophetic, it distills the longings, the confusions, and the achievements of a society into a compelling metaphor. But some plays do not show off man with accuracy or depth. They are not convincing. They lie to us and gloss over our condition. They delude us and make us forget the facts of our lives. Sometimes, if they lie with spectacular extravagance, we are lured into believing them. But unlike plays grappling with the hard truths of existence, they do not give us a sense of renewal. They idealize us, but they do not make us *self*-conscious. They do not give us back to ourselves.

Great plays focus in an artful, artificial way on the life-show that is all around us. In school, theater courses teach us drama as literature; theater on stage shows us drama as life. In *As You Like It*, Shakespeare equates illusion on the stage with life in the world: "All the world's a stage/and all the men and women merely players." But all life is not theater, even though the theatrical is part of all life. When we explore the boundary between the stage world and the real world, the questions of good roles and bad roles, of performance and authenticity dominate the inquiry. To understand the life of the stage is to confront the drama of culture. In both, we find Man making scenes, acting out his problems, manipulating sets, props, costumes, gestures, and language to reveal and conceal himself. The study of each illuminates the other.

We do not think of ourselves as theatrical. We say theater on stage is "make-believe"; the world outside is "real." We do not see ourselves as actors, but the very concept of *personality* has its roots in the Latin *persona*—a dramatic mask. Actors are signs: they give off messages with their bodies, their voices, and their words. They manipulate an audience for the required emotion; they disguise themselves in roles. They assume identities before our eyes.

So do we.

The stage elevates our daily, private "performances" to art. Our language tells us how unwittingly theatrical we are. Stage and life intermingle. People who *"play* it cool" are sometimes accused of *"showing* off." They are "making a *spectacle* of themselves," exhibiting a façade, an image, a style. We say they are *"playing* a *role."* This is part of their emotional *"make-up."* Sometimes, they perform so well that we are not sure if they are "for real"; their character might be a *"put-on."* If they are too tired to make the effort, they are *"played out."* But, if they *"act* up" or *"act* out" their inner life to us, they are *"making* a *scene."* We say: "Don't be so *dramatic."* If the person does this often, it's the same old *"routine,"* a *"number,"* a *"bit."* Throwing a *show* is just done for *effect.*

Actions also conceal and reveal. Usually, people don't explain who they are and what they really want. The clues to their real intentions are not all verbal. Their costumes, their faces, their tones of voice "give them away."

We have to pay attention to the set ("the background"), the props, the tones of scenes. The tension between them is the real "drama."

PLAY-WORDS
WORD-PLAYS

ACT: from the Latin <u>actus</u>, a doing, playing a part, dramatic action, act of a piece, and <u>actum</u>, public transaction. . . .

act-up   act-out   act-on   acting

ACTOR: from Latin. Doer, actor in a play, speaker, prosecutor, agent

dramatic   dramatize

DRAMA: from Latin <u>drāma</u>, Greek <u>drâma-at</u>: deed, action, play (especially tragedy) Formed on <u>dran</u>, to act, do

play a role   play the game   play the part

PLAY: exercise oneself, spec. by way of diversion (a game); perform on (a musical instrument). Old English: move swiftly, briskly, freely; act a character of (fourteenth century)

performing   performance

PERFORM: from the French <u>parfournir</u>, to accomplish completely

make-up   make a scene   make the scene

show-off   show-up   show-place

SHOW: to look at, examine. Old English: cause to be seen; make known, explain, exhibit, point out

stage   staged   set the stage

STAGE: from the Old French <u>estage</u>, dwelling, stay, situation. Also Roman <u>staticum</u>; standing-place, position

scenario   scenic   scenery

SCENE: from the Latin <u>scaena, scena</u>; stage, scene. Greek <u>skene</u>, tent, booth, stage, scene. Related to <u>skia</u>, shadow

The playwright knows his theme and his ending, and builds his scenes toward clarifying them. His scenes give information, expose character, and suggest ideas. He paints his picture with objects, movements, and sound. He groups his actors in significant relation to each other and "sets the stage" for action that will tell his story and analyze society. Each scene creates a pressure to which the characters react, and, gradually, deepens our knowledge of them and their world.

The life-performer, on the other hand, has only a sense of an ending, but he is part of a culture whose institutions try to write his scenario, creating scenes which attempt to forecast his future and flesh out history. He is continually being placed in cultural scenes in which special performances are demanded and in which his position is clearly blocked. The corporate ladder, the military chain of command, the classroom represent both ground plans for action and prompt-books for required responses. Within these environments, the life-performer tries to construct his image for the public. Sometimes he needs help (public relations) ; but the adept life-performer has a sense of timing, symbolic gestures, and setting with which he impresses people and conveys an idea of himself and what he stands for. His scenes are often staged and done for effect.

By "making a scene," emotion is clearly visible; people have to react to it, and this reaction tells us their mood. We remember images after we forget words.

Hamlet is involved in both stage-play and life-performance. His "madness" is at first a show: "by indirection to find directions out." But the reader or spectator watches him rehearse the players and set the stage for an image which prophesies the King's crime.

> ... *The play's the thing*
> *Wherein I'll catch the conscience of the King.*

Hamlet wants to make the source of Denmark's sickness visible, so that it can be cured. Scenes have the ability to catch the conscience of an audience. The vision—the *presence* of an irresistible truth—can move a spectator to action. Saint Francis of Assisi taught Christianity by dramatizing it. Images transcend intellectual knowledge; they speak to the heart. Saint Francis's acts of faith were not only gestures of self-renewal but an education for the illiterate masses. He went among the people; he made his faith a public event. Saint Francis said: "All brothers ought to preach by their actions." These scenes were graphic *demonstrations*. They communicated directly in vivid images. After eating too much, he had himself dragged through the town square on a rope saying: "Behold the glutton!" On his deathbed, he asked to be stripped naked and laid on the ground "to wrestle naked with the naked enemy." His presence and his performance were convincing; they carried audiences away from themselves and into a startling new understanding of faith. The exaggeration of these scenes, their contrast with normal life, made them a symbolic exhibition of belief and gave them undeniable force. The Church was not different from life; it *was* life.

Outdoors, Saint Francis of Assisi made natural an impulse which the priests—the first actors—had been contriving for centuries inside the Church. The earliest record of the Church structuring a scene is from Bishop Ethelwold in the *Concordia Regularis* (ninth century).

> *While the third lesson is being chanted, let four brethren*
> *vest themselves. Let one of these, vested in an alb, enter as*
> *though to take part in the service, and let him approach*
> *the sepulchre without attracting attention and sit there*
> *quietly with a palm in his hand. This brother is to play an*
> *angel. The sepulchre is represented by the altar. ...*
> *While the third respond is chanted, let the remaining*
> *follow and let them all, vested in copes, bearing in their*
> *hands thuribles with incense, and stepping delicately as*
> *those who seek something, approach the sepulchre. These*

*things are done in imitation of the angel sitting in the
monument and the women whose spices come to anoint
the body of Jesus. When, therefore, he who sits there beholds
the three approaching him like folk lost and seeking
something, let him begin in a dulcet voice of medium pitch
to sing* Quem Quaeritis. *And when he has sung it to the end
in unison,* Ihesu Nazarennum. . . .

*At the word of bidding let the one sitting there and,
as if recalling them, say the anthem,* Videte and Venite
Locum. *And saying this, let them rise and lift the veil and
show them the place bare of the cross, but only the cloths
laid there in which the cross was wrapped. And when
they have seen this, let them set down the thuribles which
they bare in that sepulchre, and take the strate that the
Lord has risen and is no longer wrapped therein, let them
sing the anthem,* Surrexit Dominus de Sepulchro. *When
the anthem is done, let the prior, sharing in their gladness
at the triumph of our King, in that, having vanquished
death, He rose again, begin the hymn* Te Deum Laudamus.
And this begun, all the bells chime out together. . . .

Saint Francis's scenes were more direct and outrageous
than this. His enactments were living proof of the sacra-
mental purity of life. As with Hamlet, his scenes were intended to shame the community and to force it to reconsider
its deeds. The strength of all these performances is their
physical immediacy. They provide a setting in which the
social sickness and the spiritual need can be seen. Spiritual
presence cannot be dismissed as easily as facts and figures.
This is the logic of guerrilla theater: the sudden shock of
recognition. Frantz Fanon, after the shooting of three
Martinicans by the French national police, said: "They
[the people] should use the victims . . . they should air
them, and parade them through the villages and cities in
open trucks. . . . They should shout at the people, 'Look at
the work of the colonialists.' "

This kind of direct, informational scene is carried out
in our society. "Sit-in," "Be-in" are *acts*; scenes which make
a point and a problem visible. They demonstrate.

**DANIEL BERRIGAN, SJ. How do we help Americans
get born, get going, get moving in a direction, re-
covering of what the Greeks would call the true
way? . . . It does seem to me that actors, with their
moral passion, and their bodily gestures, are in a
certain place with regard to the spirit. . . . They are
creating and communicating, light around their
bodies, the light of the spirit of man.**

PHILIP BERRIGAN. These are not times for building justice; these are times for confronting injustice. This, we feel, is the number one item of business—to confront the entrenchment, the massive complex injustice of our country. And to confront it justly, non-violently, and with maximum exposure of oneself and one's future.

Whenever we *"make* a scene" or *"make* a protest," we are constructing an image. The individual turns himself into theater, choosing to dramatize a problem, to "bring it out in the open." He evokes ideas larger than his own personality. He wants, as does the playwright, to make sure the public gets his message. Sometimes he has to spell it out.

In life as in plays, statement is never as powerful as implication. Whenever the audience discovers the meaning for themselves, the excitement and education are deeper and more lasting. Through the articulate energy contained in the scene and transmitted by the players, the viewer makes connections with society and his own emotional life. The scene functions as a metaphor, inspiring thought and interpretation. The spectator remembers instead of forgetting. We "read things into it." We say the scene was "compelling"; we got "caught up in it"; we became "*involved.*"

The *place* where actions occur often makes the point, no matter where the dialogue rambles. The environment counterpoints the words. The murky parapets of Elsinore, where voices call out into the darkness, "Who goes there?" foreshadow Hamlet's moral dilemma. The barren dream landscape of *Waiting for Godot* establishes the reasons why people play games and develop routines. The success of these images depends on many things: the performer, the subject matter, the total environment of the play.

Making a scene on stage is considered a "legitimate" means for discovering truth; making a scene in life is not. Americans are trained from birth not "to make a scene" or "act up" because "it won't *look* good." But often, it is only in these public scenes that the deepest frustrations and real failures of the parents and the child can be imagined. These scenes are a survival tactic.

JERRY RUBIN AT HUAC. The Yippies love HUAC. For us it is a costume ball: a chance to project to the children of the world our secret fantasies. What a gas it was to see the headline, "HUAC BARS SANTA CLAUS." HUAC is bullshit; it has no power.

A scene in life is the litmus paper of experience, a test which shows both the society's health and its sickness, which raises to public consciousness the invisible forces behind personality and social problems. The appeal and importance of a scene is that it is *undeniable*. The event occurs before our eyes. The actuality—and the prophecy—are witnessed. This has a visceral effect. We get "vibrations." If positive, we say we are "touched" by it, "turned on." If negative, we are "turned off." Either way, the individual has been *moved* and is conscious of his spiritual *re-action*.

Life-scenes can haunt us. Framed and controlled with a sense of public occasion or the drama of place, they become images which cannot be clicked off as easily as television.

These scenes generate excitement in everyday experience and make a comment on it. They make the commonplace vivid. By organizing experience into coherent images, the scenes unwittingly have a strong effect on the human brain. Nigel Calder has written:

Mild excitement is necessary for the brain to work at its most efficient; also when arousal becomes intense emotion, efficiency falls off sharply. The expressions "blind with rage," "rigid with fear" are not fanciful, while a person exposed to more troubles than he can cope with may simply fall asleep.—The Mind of Man

Scenes distance a dilemma while making the spectators aware of it. They have the ability to renew our energy and clarify our sense of purpose and understanding.

ALLEN GINSBERG ON DEMONSTRATIONS. A Demonstration is a theatrical production. The life style, energy and joy of the demonstration can be made into an exemplary spectacle of how to handle situations of anxiety and fear/threat.

The image of solidarity—the conviction of the performance—impresses the spectator and reinforces the belief of the participant. These scenes can touch a demonic or benevolent spiritual need in a culture. As a radical of the right trying to get public attention and make his ideas visible. Adolf Hitler's success rested heavily on his theatrical instinct. Hitler understood the impact of a staged presentation and the effect of direct scenic power on the imagination. Obsessed with theatrical performance, his intuitions about changing public ideas are important.

TIMING. At night [the people] succumb more easily to the dominating force of a stronger will. For, in truth, every meeting represents a wrestling between two opposing forces. The superior oratorical art of a dominating preacher will succeed more easily in winning to the new will people who have themselves experienced a weakening of their force of resistance in the most natural way than those who are still in full possession of their mental tension and will. The same purpose, after all, is served by the artificially made and yet mysterious twilight of Catholic churches, the burning lamps, incense, censers.

In this wrestling bout of the speaker with the adversaries he wants to convert, he will gradually achieve that wonderful sensitivity to the psychological requirements of propaganda, which the writer almost always lacks. Hence, the written word in

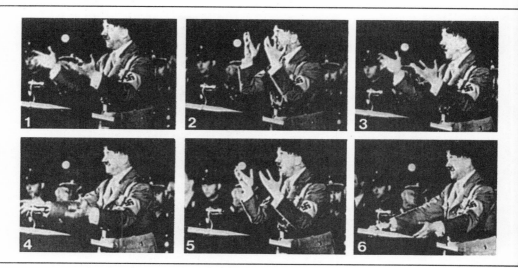

its limited effect will in general serve more to retain, reinforce, to deepen a point of view that is already present. Really great historical changes are not induced by the written word, but at most accompanied by it. . . .—Mein Kampf

Public scenes, like staged ones, are a shared experience. This bond is gratifying, and can be manipulated for actions either good or bad. Hitler excoriated the well-mannered, sleepy political meetings of his enemies; he wanted to make a scene which was unforgettable, which excited and agitated his audience.

THE MASS MEETING. The mass meeting is also necessary for the reason that in it the individual who at first, while becoming a supporter of a young movement, feels lonely and easily succumbs to the fear of being alone, for the first time gets the picture of a larger community which in most people has a strengthening, encouraging effect. . . . He is swept away by three or four thousand others into the mighty effect of suggestive intoxication and enthusiasm when the visible success and agreement of thousands confirm to him the rightness of the new doctrine and for the first time around doubt in the truth of his previous conviction—then he himself has succumbed to the magic influence of what we designate as "mass suggestion." The will, the long-

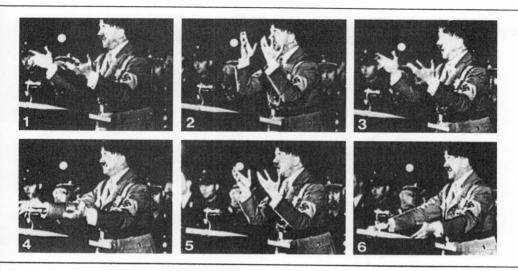

ing and also the power of thousands are accumulated in every individual . . . .—Mein Kampf

In *Mein Kampf*, Hitler significantly extends into the public arena the theater's "magic"; its ability to transport us, to captivate the imagination with mythic spectacles that overcome time.

On stage and in life, scenes must be framed. All magicians have to plan their tricks and anticipate their audience. Success depends on their "professionalism." This is a relative term; it depends on the circumstances and goals of the performer. What the actor wants to show and how he shows it reveal his talent and his purpose. Hitler paid meticulous attention to the details of public performance: banners and insignia were chosen with a director's sense of the symbolic and emotional effects of color on an audience.

COLOR. . . . We chose the red color of our posters after careful and thorough reflection, in order to provoke the Left, to drive them to indignation and lead them to attend our meetings if only to break them up, in order to have some chance to speak to the people.—Mein Kampf

The spectator is in the presence of energy; and that experience is heightened and dramatized by the delivery, the background, the mood of the audience. The scene is intended to seize the imagination. The speaker is, by definition, an

actor. He embodies a point of view. The scene he creates
from the podium has an immediate impact and also carries
a sense of anticipation about the future. Like stage-play, the
best life-performances are specific and prophetic.

These direct scenes do not disguise their theatrical flair.
The performers want to draw attention to themselves: to
outrage and to educate. They make a spectacle of their
belief. Their costumes, the repetition of dramatic gestures
(peace signs, clenched fists, salutes, handshakes), coor-
dinated public scenes are intended as a continual visual
reminder of their interpretation of social order and a higher
moral truth. Direct scenes can instruct by pleasing. Hu-

morous scenes expose cultural contradictions. Dramatic contrast needs no words to explain it. Everything can be turned into props.

The emphasis, as with all good theater, is to show, not tell. Every scene is a contest of will. Whether the public scenes set spiritual force against material force (the riots at Kent State, the Berrigans, Gandhi, the Yippies) or the reverse (police blockade, military riot-control), there is a sense of physical danger. This tension is crucial to the playwright as well as to the public performer. The life/death struggle is spellbinding. The beauty of the performance is built partially around fear: Antigone, Oedipus, Lear, Wozzeck, a moonshot. Even the language of stage performance implies the sense of ultimate struggle. Success on stage is measured as conquest: "I killed them!" "I knocked 'em dead!"; failure as death: "I died out there!" "I bombed out!" Great performances on stage or in public are a kind

of ecstasy. The performer "opens himself up," "gives it everything he's got," "lays it on the line." On stage, this intimate expending of energy exhibits a frightening vulnerability: it is a religious, almost sacrificial act.

The same spontaneous, irrational momentum of a performance that awes a theater audience can overwhelm at public scenes. In earlier centuries, public scenes were mostly local events. With television, however, scenes from all over the world can be played out in the home. Even if this reduces the tactile quality of the experience, it extends its range. It makes the performer more conscious of being seen and more cagey about what he wants to show. Today, press conferences, news interviews, official outings are the events for which both the public and the heads of state are "prepared." Everyone makes his own setting. We talk of "setting ourselves up" in business; women "make themselves up," and men "set the stage" for a seduction. We allow ourselves to be seen in "a certain light."

In the Middle Ages, it was a strange, unique experience to come upon a dramatic figure like Saint Francis of Assisi. Now, TV makes public scenes a daily occurrence. The modern viewer is bombarded with more imagery of action than ever before in man's history.

ABBIE HOFFMAN AT CHICAGO. Our actions in Chicago established a brilliant figure-ground relationship. The rhetoric of the Convention was allotted the fifty minutes of the hour, we were given the ten or less usually reserved for the commercials. We were an advertisement for the revolution. We were a high degree of involvement played out against the dull field of establishment rhetoric. Watching the Convention play out its boring drama, one could not help but be conscious of the revolution being played out in the streets.

That underlying tension builds up and the viewer becomes totally involved in what we are doing EVEN IF HE CANNOT SEE OR EXPERIENCE IT DIRECTLY. He creates the Yippies, the cops and other participants in his own image. He constructs his own play. He fabricates his own myth. Even if the media decided on a total blackout of our activities, our message would have gotten through and perhaps with even more power. All people had to know what was that America's children were getting slaughtered in the streets of Chicago and the networks were refusing to show it. WE CAN NEVER BE SHUT OUT. . . .

Hoffman's analysis of his public performance is shrewd but misguided. As a "life-actor" (his term for himself), he sometimes misunderstands media saturation. As with any TV performer, his act can be overexposed. His scenes lose their surprise and shock. The unexpected becomes expected. Television has the weird, deadly ability of giving us experience without risk. In other eras, images on stage were banned because their view of society was offensive or incendiary. (Under Cromwell's Protectorate, 1653–1658, English playhouses were burned and no public performances of stage plays allowed.) Television magnifies the problem. To maintain their power and control, modern governments must eliminate public expression of discontent. President Nixon speaks of wiping out student protest: "We have the power to strike back, if need be, and to prevail. The nation has survived other attempts at insurrection. We can survive this." Vice-President Agnew attacks the media, saying: "Normality has become the nemesis of network news. Now the upshot of all this controversy is that a narrow and distorted *picture* of America emerges from the television news." Authority is worried about the picture such scenes paint. Things must seem normal or "it won't look good." Government would eliminate (jail, kill, discredit) those who make public scenes. Out of sight, out of mind.

The 1968 Chicago convention proved Hoffman's tactics to be only partially successful; the Chicago Conspiracy Trial illustrated their severe limitation. If the performance is reported but not *seen* (Bobby Seale bound and gagged in the courtroom), its impact is lost on the public. Moral fervor must be *exhibited*. Frustration at not being able to get a hearing, or failure to communicate, can lead to attempts to capture the public's attention by more violent

means: bombings, immolations, kidnapings. On television and in newsprint, they all have the same weight. But life-performances, like stage scenes, must be tested for their spiritual depth and integrity.

It would be wrong to think that scenes are acted out on

the public only by frustrated minorities and that the information given out by playwrights or public performances is solely a call to revolution. Historically, the reverse is truer. Most public theater has been staged by the society's leaders on the public: coronations, ceremonies of state, tableaux of manners and wealth. The intention of these scenes is not to shock but to dazzle; not to make the public question but accept. The drama and conviction in these kinds of scenes lie in their size and elaborate contrivance. They are frank displays of power, authority, position, and wealth.

A courtier's clothes were a sign of his role, "setting" him off from the rest of the world. Walking the streets of London or Paris, he would always stand out. Court life ritualized the actor-audience relationship, just as stage performances try to do. Louis XIV's Versailles was built without a theater. It didn't need one. Life there was a continual performance.

The courtier had his own toilet to make, which, even if it did not include washing, meant an elaborate powdering and prinking, before attending his patron's levee and following him to that of the King.

In the King's room the day began at about a quarter to eight, when the First Valet de Chambre, who had slept in the room, would dismantle and put away his bed; if it was winter, the two porte-bûchon du roi, *the royal faggot-bearers, would next make their appearance to light the King's fire, followed a minute or two later by the King's watchmaker to wind up the royal watch. From a side door would enter the royal wigmaker, coming from the room in which the King's wigs reposed, each on its pedestal, in glass-fronted wardrobes—hunting wigs, council wigs, evening wigs, walking wigs. . . .*

On the first stroke of eight his valet would wake him, and the exciting news that His Majesty was awake would pass into the closely packed ante-room to set the courtiers rustling like a field of ripe corn in a summer breeze. At the same moment the First Physician and the first surgeon entered the room, together with the King's old Nurse, who went up to the bed, kissed him, and asked him how he slept, whilst the two medical men rubbed the King down and changed his shirt. At a quarter-past eight the Grand Chamberlain was admitted together with those courtiers who had the coveted grandes entrées *and Louis was presented with Holy Water. Now was the time to ask the King a favor.*

When the moment came for him to put on his shirt, that garment would be handed to the senior person present by the First Valet, and the man so favored would then hand it to the King. . . . Having dressed, the King then knelt down at his bed and said his prayers, all ecclesiastics in attendance kneeling down at the same time, but the lay

*courtiers remaining standing; after which he went into
his private rooms, followed by the most exalted of the
court only. . . .—W. H. LEWIS, The Splendid Century*

The day was divided into little dramatic scenes. From
the King's awakening, he is *acting*. His famous dictum *L'état
c'est moi* makes his theatrical intention clear. He becomes
the metaphor of a nation. Since all power is vested in him,
he must make a spectacle of his grandeur and authority.
His performance demands certain specific responses from
his audience—the court. Both parts of the theatrical equation are needed for the event to take place: the King's power
and freedom, the audience's privilege and subservience.
Every action in the court reinforces conformity, binding
the audience to the King's power. But the King is continually on *show*.

*If Louis was dining au public, any decently dressed person
could witness him doing so, and to drive out from Paris
to Versailles to see the King eat was a popular form of
entertainment.—W. H. LEWIS*

Performances of this same general nature are a feature
of every human society, seemingly an essential function of
communal life. Their styles vary with the cultural taste
and emotional needs of the members of the community.
They are the means by which authority personifies itself,
conveying an idea of itself not by words but by images and
actions.

**PERSONIFICATION. . . . pinpoints in terms of psy-
chology, drama, and technique the system leading
from the acquisition of power, to the individual interpretation of it, to the "stage setting" for the hero,
to the preparation of the crowd through propaganda, to the weaving of the myth, to the incarnation of the individual, to the gradual merging of the
sign-given group with the sign-giving demigod.—**
JEAN LACOUTURE, The Demigods

The regularity and directness of spectacles of state is com-
forting to the public. They become participants in the state's
pageantry. The Government reinforces its control and its
majesty by these familiar productions of pomp and cir-
cumstance. As on stage, the community between the public
actor and the audience touches deep emotions and releases
unknown energies in both. These are visible demonstrations of power in benign action. Symbols that surround the
setting take on a new life and importance.

The productions of state are often deliberately staged; some leaders are coached by stage actors to enhance their performance (Hitler, Eisenhower, LBJ, Nixon). The public sees their leaders only in "set" surroundings. As in all theater, the backdrop defines and highlights the figure in front of it. As Erving Goffman writes in *The Presentation of Self in Everyday Life*, "Queen Victoria enforced the rule that anyone seeing her approach when she was driving her pony-cart on the palace grounds should turn his head or walk in another direction." Governments also manipulate their image in such a way to create a mood and a sense of mission.

Hitler, obsessed with theater and architecture, made a science of his "look." "My surroundings must look magnificent," he told his architect Albert Speer. "Then my simplicity makes a striking effect." Hitler had a stage-set designer create diplomatic dress and military medals for his Reich; and Speer created monuments whose size were a barometer of Hitler's view of himself in history.

BUILDING THE NUREMBERG STADIUM. . . . Within this enormous tract, an area of 3,400 by 2,300 feet was set aside where the army could practice minor maneuvers. By contrast, the grandiose area of the palace of King Darius I and Xerxes in Persepolis (5th Century B.C.) had embraced only 1,500 by 900 feet. Stands 48 feet high were to surround the area, providing seats for a hundred and sixty thousand spectators. Twenty-four towers over a hundred and thirty feet in height were to punctuate these stands; in the middle was a platform for guests of honor which was to be crowned by a sculpture of a woman. In A.D. 64 Nero erected on the Capitol a colossal figure 119 feet high. The Statue of Liberty in New York is 151 feet high; our statue was to be 46 feet higher. . . . The marchfield opened out into a processional avenue a mile and a quarter long. . . . On the right rose a flight of stairs from which Hitler, flanked by his generals, would review such parades. Opposite was a colonnade where the flags of the regiments would be displayed. . . .—ALBERT SPEER, Inside the Third Reich

---

Hitler's explanation of the architecture is pertinent. "Why always the biggest? I do this to restore to each individual German his self-respect. In a hundred areas I want to say to the individual: We are not inferior; on the contrary, we are the complete equals of every nation." Speer himself came to understand the full meaning behind Hitler's theatrical settings. "He wanted the biggest of everything to glorify his works and magnify his pride. These monuments were an assertion of his claim to world dominion *long before he dared to voice any such intention even to his closest associates.*"

The playwright knows that the objects which surround an individual reveal him: both the facts of his life and his dream of what it should be. He also knows that *position* on stage implies *relation*: people group themselves in ways symbolic of their attitude. The Greek tragic hero is not only separated from the chorus by the timbre of his voice, but by his physical isolation. In *King Lear*, Cordelia's relationship to her sisters is not only discussed, it can be shown by how they are positioned around her.

Because public performance is as artificial as a playwright's script, the public must look beneath the surface to discover its real meaning and purpose. A performance may seem sincere, but that does not mean it is truthful. At the same time, what is moving is not necessarily profound.

MAGIC OF THE MASSES. Then after the War, I experienced a mass demonstration of the Marxists. . . . A sea of red flags, red scarves and red flowers gave to this demonstration . . . an aspect that was gigantic from a purely external point of view. I myself could feel and understand how easily the mass of the people succumbs to the suggestive magic of a spectacle so grandiose in effect.—Mein Kampf

NKRUMAH DESCRIBES BECOMING PREMIER. No general could have been prouder of his Army. . . . In the amphitheater, which is the cradle of my party, the customary rite of expiation was deemed appropriate: a lamb was sacrificed and I plunged my bare foot into its blood seven times to purify myself of prison.

CONOR CRUISE O'BRIEN ON NKRUMAH'S PER-FORMANCE. Kwame Nkrumah was a splendid actor, which made it difficult to talk to him because he tended to "overact," as if his expression . . . had to be vehement enough to reach a vast audience. . . . I had several opportunities to admire his performance on the stage of Parliament, with his private herald chanting his praises in the corridors and his eight spokesmen with their gold-headed halberds. . . . The audience warmed to him, the way it does in the theater, not at a political rally. It made me think of those Italian soldiers who responded to the sword-waving exhortations of their commander, not budging from their trenches, with a chorus of "Bravo! Bravissimo!"

In all these public scenes, the boundary between actor and audience is more ambiguous than it seems. The roles in a life-performance continually change. While a government and its leaders frame scenes to which the public will respond, the public's response gives the event its validity. A motorcade down empty streets would be as meaningless as a stage performance without an audience. The spectators—the "audience"—discover a sense of their own power through the ruling authority who has created the occasion. This accounts for the reverence with which crowds often treat public figures and great stage performers. In public spectacles, the crowd assumes a larger identity and new destiny through their imaginative bond with the leader. On stage, the performer's life-giving quality allows an audience to feel not only for him, but *through* him. Conscious of being observed, the audience acts in a certain way. The will of the audience as well as the leader is on show. The audience is the scenery of the spectacle. But the audience also feels itself an agent, a doer (i.e., an actor) in the event, offering a reassuring, regenerative image of unity to the leader, just as the leader is offering a reassuring image of power and direction to the audience. This becomes not only an act of faith (going to the people, the people turning out for the event), but a means of deepening the mutual dependence. The religious quality of the audience-actor relationship is important. The audience wants to believe, to confirm its role, as well as the power and quality of those they applaud. Their sense of betrayal in political scenes comes from the mistaken idea that politics is not performance.

THE AUDIENCE AND ILLUSION. In the case of dramatized politics there is also, especially in moments of great danger, a strong wish to believe in the spectacle as real: identification with a national leader or spokesman represses any intimation that he may be playing a part in the theatrical sense. Even when it was proved—as for example in the case of Adlai Stevenson on the Bay of Pigs crisis—that an actor's lines belonged strictly to the world of fiction, a wide public wished to forget this and resented, and still resents, any reference to the fact, very much as the religious public may resent any reference to bogus miracles. It is not that the public any longer argues for the reality of the miracle; it is just that references to it wound the public of its essential piety, in its will to believe, and in its dignity.—CONOR CRUISE O'BRIEN

Mao Tse-tung's Chinese cultural revolution epitomizes the life-performance as a means of establishing the sense of the leader's immortal, heroic stature. It also forces the Chinese public to discover the purpose and direction of the revolution by participating in the dramatic new imagery of a revolutionary society. The spectacles Mao stages incarnate the revolutionary mythology behind his thought: tableaux which acknowledge Mao's vision of China, "her great history, staggering population and vast land—which render her immune to the dangers of the contemporary world and to the limitations of human existence" (Robert J. Lifton, *Revolutionary Immortality*). In 1966, with the establishment of the Red Guard—an attempt to bind the young to the revolution and insure their continued performance for it—Mao staged the now-famous Dawn Scene.

MAO'S DAWN SCENE. . . . a million people gathered in the great square singing "The East Is Red." Mao Tse-tung powerful in his presence though walking slowly and stiffly (thereby encouraging rumors of severe illness), then moving out among the masses on the arm of a teenage girl—went further and spoke of a "new community." I would suggest that this new community, in a symbolic sense, is a community of immortals—of men, women and children entering into a new relationship with the eternal revolutionary process. An event of this kind is meant to convey a blending of the immortal cultural and racial substance of the Chinese as people with the equally immortal Communist revolution. . . .—ROBERT J. LIFTON, Revolutionary Immortality

The thrust of the society is on show: the spectacle of its finest dreams is given lavish attention and detail. The Chinese image emphasizes the action of the people: the freedom through struggle and a new community of revolutionary workers. The American images stress teamwork: the isolation of technological power from the public; the unquestioning acceptance of technology's destiny and men's subservience to the machinery; freedom which has more to do with technological domination and passive security than struggle. Both types of spectacle paint direct, vivid pictures by the governments for their cultures, cutting through the confusions, ignorance, and uncertainty of the people to justify and sustain their leadership.

MAO TSE-TUNG AND THE AUDIENCE. "Apart from their other characteristics, China's 600 million people have two remarkable peculiarities: they are, first of all, poor, and secondly blank. That may seem like a bad thing. But it is really a good thing. Poor people want change, want to do things, want revolution. A clean sheet of paper has no blotches, and so the newest and most beautiful words can be written on it."—ROBERT J. LIFTON, Revolutionary Immortality

Making a scene is a form of advertising. Mao's posters or the spectacular military displays communicate the idea of a Communist state and the nature of revolutionary work. In a capitalist society, advertising becomes a flamboyant production, and an equally powerful institution of social control which paints pictures of products. This itself is a political act. Advertising forces the public to define itself as a consumer and stimulates new needs. Products are dramatized. The promotional task of advertising is the same as the propaganda for government: "(1) to get *Attention*; (2) to hold *Interest*; (3) to arouse *Desire*; and (4) to obtain *Action*" (*Basic Marketing: A Managerial Approach*, E. Jerome McCarthy). One society is promoting social change; the other, social acceptance.

In America, objects have a theatrical life of their own. Advertising stages products for consumption: set off in special displays, packaged in carefully designed containers, associated with familiar songs and catch phrases, the object is always made to seem dramatically new and alluring. Industry tries to elevate the product into a symbol (brand name) and find a trade-mark which will make it memorable: a means of defeating competition and sustaining public faith. Mass production demands mass consumption; and the goal of advertising is the *adoption* of objects, not ideas. The theatrical process of advertising envelops us; the product is sold and surrounded by artifice. Entertainers endorse objects; the objects themselves can be animated to sing and dance for us on television. Advertisers create entire personalities around their product. When we consume, we are not only acquiring the object, but a complete fictional world of advertised associations. Smoke Marlboro and return to the cowboy's pastoral, heroic world. Use Wild Root Creme Oil and you'll get the girls. Cook with Spatini Spaghetti and you'll be loved ("a *keess* in the *keetchen*"). Scour the floor with Ajax and you'll have the purifying magic and power of a white knight. Implied in

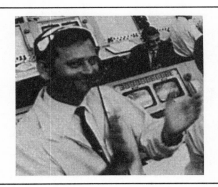

every campaign is an idealization of life through the product, a new and improved existence through acquisition. "Our economy depends upon our willingness to turn to things rather than people for gratification, to symbols rather than our bodies. The gross national product will reach its highest point when the material object can be interpolated between every itch and its scratch" (Philip Slater, *The Pursuit of Loneliness*).

Mao's Dawn Scene contains a prophecy: the spectacle of millions of people working together for Mao and the revolution he has led. The image, its size and control, conveys a sense of immortality—the struggle and revolutionary principles imbued in the Chinese people who will carry on the revolution even after Mao's death.

In America, a technological society, the scenes which captivate the public and draw the widest attention are

those which illustrate the immortality of human will and intelligence through a benevolent technology. The space program is a stunning, extravagant display carrying beneath the drama of its mechanical ingenuity and the daredevil danger facing the spacemen, the yearning of a materialist culture to transcend itself through objects. In both cases, the imagery is overwhelming; the spectator is awed by the imposing dream.

ADVERTISING'S SILENT MESSAGE. If the economic effect is to make the purchaser like what he buys, the social effect is in a parallel but broader sense, to make the individual like what he gets—to enforce already existing attitudes, to diminish the range and variety of choices, and in terms of abundance to exalt the materialistic virtues of consumption.—DAVID M. POTTER, People of Plenty

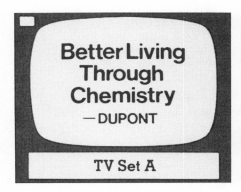

AND NOW A WORD FROM OUR SPONSOR. The average child will have received more hours of "instruction" from television by the time he enters first grade than the number of hours he will later spend in college classrooms earning a B.A. degree. By the time he is a teenager he will have spent from 15,000 to 20,000 hours with the television set and seen anywhere from 250,000 to 500,000 commercials.—NICHOLAS JOHNSON, Federal Communications Commissioner, 1971

In a culture whose economy functions on such a theatrical display of possession, it is not surprising that the society makes a ceremonial exhibition of consumption. Wealth is to be shown off; and honored as a costume which marks rank, leisure, and good taste. Thorstein Veblen coined the term "conspicuous consumption" to explain this pattern of American materialism: "The only practicable means of impressing one's pecuniary ability on these unsympathetic observers of one's everyday life is an unremitting demonstration of ability to pay." But Sir Epicure Mammon in Ben Jonson's *The Alchemist* dramatized the theatrical impulse

behind accumulation in the new wealth of the Elizabethan
Age. "Be rich/This day you shall be spectatitissimi." Mammon wants to turn wealth into an awe-inspiring stage
event: a production which commands immediate respect
from any audience that encounters it. Sir Epicure spins the
same fantasy as modern advertising: broadcasting a faith
in the immortality of objects and the spiritual satisfaction
of consumption. What kind of man reads *Playboy*? The
same kind who once dreamed of impossible sensual pleasure:

And I will eat these broths with spoons of amber,
Headed with diamond and carbuncle.
My foot-boy shall eat pheasants, calver'd salmons,
Knots, godwits, lampreys: I myself will have
The beards of barbels served, instead of salads;
Oil'd mushrooms; and the swelling unctuous paps
Of a fat pregnant sow, newly cut off. . . .
—BEN JONSON, The Alchemist

The obsession with consumption takes on a sexual passion:
both Mammon and the advertiser confuse acquisition with
Eros, moral value with financial worth.

PRODUCTS AS PENIS POWER.
Epicure Mammon:
She shall feel gold, taste gold, hear gold,
sleep gold;
Nay we will concubere gold:
I will be puissant.

SEX AND SALESMANSHIP. The call of the Wild
Streak: It's irresistible. Now! The first complete kit
to fashion-streak your hair. Like all good lures, the
Wild Streak is beautifully simple. No retouching
for up to six seductive months. Why hide the secret
hidden inside of you? Answer the call of the Wild
Streak. You're not the type to be timid. And this is
no time to be tame.—Cosmopolitan Magazine

The economic displays of the culture are scenes which
also create an invisible, but real sense of humiliation.
"Since the consumption of these more excellent goods is an
evidence of wealth, it becomes honorific," writes Veblen.
"Conversely, the failure to consume in due quantity and
quality becomes a mask of inferiority and demerit." Advertising is an institution selling a way of life: possession

is equated with freedom and happiness. It does not recognize poverty since it is staging tableaux of national abundance. But the poor are attracted and frustrated by these scenes. Need is stimulated; but satisfaction stalled. The scenes are convincing; and, in a society dedicated to the aggrandizement of wealth, the audience wants to believe the fantasies that accompany it. There is a scenario of action built into each spectacular advertisement. Since the poor are continually bombarded with new "needs," they must work harder within the system to afford them. The poor assume roles in the economy of which they are not even aware. Victims of the social ethic, they nonetheless espouse the values which oppress them. They are hamstrung in an endless competition ("Keeping up with the Joneses") which they can never win. In the face of this continual reminder of humiliation and hopeless contest, the other alternative is crime, where the business ethic of pluck 'n luck is turned on its head.

If advertising structures an invisible pressure, a subtext for capitalism's economic drama, making scenes can also be a conscious, bravura act of intimidation. The gesture reveals as much about the doer as the victim. Sometimes, governments (with the leaders scrupulously invisible) stage scenes which have the equivalent theatrical outrage and sense of indomitable power as Marlowe's invisible Doctor Faustus gulling the Pope. The Red Guard unleashed verbal and physical abuse on those Chinese who were in the "Five Black" categories and thought "counter-revolutionary." Besides confiscating possessions, the Guard paraded the "abusers" through the streets in dunce's caps. The theatrical gesture was a living reminder of political aims. As one Red Guard manifesto read: "We are the Red Guard of Chairman Mao. We tear up and smash old calendars, precious vases, and ancient paintings, and we put up the picture of Chairman Mao." Similarly, Hitler's SS displayed Jews. Their houses and shops were painted with yellow stars and the word JUDEN; they were forced to wear arm bands that made a mockery of their faith in public and isolated them from the community. The humiliation did more than emphasize Nazi power and political goals. Symbolically, the Jews' "acceptance" of these performances built up the public's anti-Semitic feeling about their "weakness." Treated like objects, their image of being "less than human" was continually reinforced by these government productions. The language of these scenes which reduces the participant to "dog," "pig," "swine," etc.—indicates how humanity is stripped from such confrontation. In this setting, it becomes easier to destroy.

POLITICAL BEAR-BAITING. [We must] separate
protest leaders from our society with no more regret than we should feel over discarding rotten
apples from a barrel. Harrrisburg, Pennsylvania,
1969.—SPIRO T. AGNEW

Humiliation is usually accompanied by invective. The
performer acts in such a way as to rob the spectator of his
freedom and reduce him to submission. The spectator is
caught and used in this drama. We say that these scenes

are made "at the expense" of others; and, they also increase
the performer's sense of his worth. The performer's power,
his identity, and his freedom are bolstered in proportion
to his domination of another's will.

The intensity of these scenes have the ability to repel

as well as fascinate. Passion can expose the mask of personality even in conquest. Shrewd politicians understand this and sometimes allow scenes to be made against them in order to gain public favor.

NIXON MAKES A SCENE. Nixon's advance men this fall have carefully arranged with local police to allow enough dissenters in the staging areas so the President will have his theme well illustrated as he warms to his job.—HUGH SIDEY, Life Magazine, 1970

Direct scenes are often made to confirm a sense of identity or to signal frustration at not being acknowledged. On stage, Jimmy Porter's invective in John Osborne's *Look Back in Anger* becomes a gauge of Porter's own sense of failure and inferiority. Thersites' mockery in *Troilus and Cressida*, like Nixon's mockery of the peace symbols to protesters ("They hate it when I do that"), is intended to inflict on others the emptiness they feel in themselves. As with the abusive games of Vladimir and Estragon in Beckett's *Waiting for Godot*, the intention behind the scene may vary, but the source is the same. Estragon says: "We always find something, eh, Didi, to give us the impression we exist."

ACTING OUT

We say performers act out a situation. This implies not only that the actor embodies a fictional role, but that he directs energy toward an audience—out to it. What happens "behind the scenes" is not as important as what's going on "out front." Actors, on stage and in life, are continually putting up a "front" because, as advertising has emphasized in American culture, "it's what's up front that counts."

To be an outstanding stage performer is to transform inner feeling into external form. An actor carries forward not only the through-line of the play's action, but his own spiritual transformations within the dramatic events. This is a difficult task. How does the actor touch his emotions, and how does he know how to make them subtly visible? Stanislavski, the Russian director who was the first to systematize an approach to acting, has written:

Each person evolves an external characterization out of himself from others, takes it from real or imaginary life, according to his intuition, his observation of himself and others. He draws it from his own experience of life or that of his friends, from pictures, engravings, drawings, books, stories, novels, or from some simple incident— it makes no difference. The only proviso is that while he is making this external research he must not lose his inner self.—Building a Character

Theater dramatizes man adapting to the external world, searching for a personal identity while confronting social categories. On stage and in life, we lose part of ourselves in order to discover ourselves. We wear and express the choices we have made. If they are crude or unsuggestive, if they overemphasize part of a role while overlooking another—this is still indicative of the limitations of the performer's personality.

This kind of acting is the art of approximation. Character is defined as the accretion of observed and discovered detail. A great actor can locate emotions in himself and instinctively know what emotional and physical details to show an audience. Identity on stage is forged by training, discipline, invention, observation, and endurance. A role is not arrived at easily. The actor rehearses his "character" and his style, usually without an audience or with those who will not judge him as he gropes to find a self which will be acceptable. He experiments; he prunes the image until he inhabits the character he wants to be. This is, literally, an "im*persona*tion." The performer attempts to eliminate anything that would not make him credible. The performer doesn't have to believe what he's saying to be convincing. He *becomes* the character, but to do this he must hide himself. In this kind of performance his technique is a means of evasion. A bad performance, we say, "has no life in it." It lacks energy and self-perspective. A bad actor makes us aware of the fullness possible in the dramatic role and shows how short the performance falls from the ideal. Stanislavski wrote:

It often happens that an actor has all the fine, subtle, deep feelings necessary to his part and yet may distort them beyond recognition because he conveys them through crudely prepared external physical means. When the body transmits neither the actor's feelings to me nor how he experiences them I see an out of tune, inferior instrument on which a fine musician is obliged to perform. The poor man! He struggles so hard to transmit all the shadings of emotions. The stiff keys on the piano do not yield to his touch, the unoiled pedals squeak, the strings are jangled and out of tune. All this causes an artist great effort and pain. The more complex the life of the human spirit in the part being protrayed, the more compelling and artistic should be the physical form which clothes it. . . . This makes an enormous call on our external technique, on the expressiveness of our bodily apparatus, our voice, diction, intonation, handling of words, phrases, speeches, our facial expression, plasticity of movement. To a supreme degree sensitive to the slightest twist, the subtlest turns and changes in our inner lives while on stage, they must be like the most delicate barometers, responsive to imperceptible atmospheric changes.
—Building a Character

The good performer "fleshes out" the role. He is comfortable with his character and his body; he puts an audience at ease. We say he performed "flawlessly." The idea of the character, the sense of his concreteness and conviction has been fully realized, i.e., made real. The actor was "believable," "convincing": there was no apparent self-consciousness or straining which seem forced or which "broke the spell" of his impersonation. Hamlet's advice to the players reflects Shakespeare's understanding of this delicate balance of taste and selection in the simulation of personality.

HAMLET DIRECTS. Be not too tame neither, but let your own discretion be your tutor: suit the action to the word, the word to the action; with this special observance, that you o'erstep not the modesty of nature: for anything so overdone is from the purpose of playing, whose end, both at the first and now, was and is, to hold, as 'twere, the mirror up to Nature; to show virtue her own feature, scorn her own image, and the very age and body of the time his form and pressure. Now this overdone or come tardy off, though it make the unskillful laugh, cannot but make the judicious grieve; the censure of the which one must in your allowance o'erweigh a whole theatre of others. O, there be players that I have seen play, and heard others praise, and that highly, not to speak it profanely, that neither having the accent of Christians nor the gait of Christian, pagan, nor man, have so strutted and bellowed, that I have thought some of nature's journeymen had made men, and not made them well, they imitated humanity so abominably.

To imitate is to copy. The action implies both a longing to idealize and a personal limitation: what we want to be and what we are not. The actor's success is measured on how much we *believe* him; how well he has adopted appearances and attitudes and reproduces the physical details and dialects observed in everyday life. (This approach has been carried to extremes by the Moscow Art Theatre where, in a staging of Gorki's *Lower Depths*, a real tramp was brought on in place of an actor.) The process is *artificial*; the actor makes himself into an object of art. When we speak of a "credibility gap," we mean a discrepancy between words and actions. The public performance is bad. The actors on stage or in life cannot be *believed*. They may say all the right words, they may use all the correct gestures, but something does not "ring true."

The actor may "look the part," but he can't "pull it off." His action has not been carried through in such a way that we feel he's authentic. In both stage and public perform-

ances, the actor has to feel out his audience and the needs of his scene. The audience wants to believe; but it can easily be scared. It is a courtship, where both parties are nervous. Each dramatic situation has its own emotional pattern. This varies with each culture. Sometimes a performer "comes on too strong"; the audience isn't sure "what he's getting at." If he presses himself on the audience when it wants to be lured by his presence; the actor is too "pushy." On stage, the word for this pressure is "flop-sweat." The term implies a blemish. The quality of private care is too obvious. The audience is "put off"; it does not "accept" him. The relationship is delicate. The performer must discover the rhythm of his scene, and intuitively know the rhythm of the audience. One must feed the other, or the act will not work.

There are many tricks to getting the right "effect," and "making a good impression." Make-up, props, staging all play a part in giving a performance weight and conviction.

PROJECTING AN IMAGE. . . . 'We have to be very clear on this point: that the response is to the image, not the man. . . . It's not what's there that counts, it's what's projected—carrying it one step further, it's not what he projects but rather what the voter receives. It's not the man we have to change, but rather the received impression.—JOE MC GINNISS, The Selling of the President, 1968

On stage, the good actor "projects" his character to the last seat in the auditorium. To be felt, his performance must be clearly seen and heard. Since he is acting out the situation, he is not explaining it but dramatizing it. The audience is faced with an equation of human action, in which they are given all the factors, and which they must solve. The

mystery is part of the fun and the impact of the performance. Objects can bolster this impersonation. If the stage
is too cluttered and the performer not careful about his
appearance, people might "get the wrong impression." On
the other hand, if the actor is too specific and literal about
what he's doing, his actions "leave nothing to the imagination." Carefully selected props define a character, silently
punctuating the performance, tantalizing the spectator and
inviting the imagination to play. The stage performer wants
to hint at the ideas he embodies; he wants the audience to
discover his meaning. Everything he does or wears should
reinforce the idea behind his characterization. Hamlet's
intellectual distance from experience at the beginning of
the tragedy is mirrored in the notebook in which he writes
his observations after seeing his father's ghost. The book
is the vestige of his university training, a cerebral reflex
which will soon have to be abandoned for action:

O villain, villain, smiling, damned villain!
My tables—meet it is I set it down,
(Writing) *That one may smile and smile and be a*
villain. . . .

Hamlet, of course, changes his costume to convey another idea of himself. He was "the glass of fashion and
the mould of form"; his "madness" is reflected in his di-
sheveled dress. In a real sense, he makes himself into a
prop, an object to be used, and also something to which
people must react. This method of acting out is not just a
stage process, but also effective in life-performances. To
announce the withdrawal of France from Algeria, Charles
de Gaulle put on his military uniform for the first time in
a decade. France's war hero was reinforcing the dignity
of his decision, and reminding the public of the past and
the faith they had always placed in him.

**NIXON'S COSTUME. His rigid wall of decorum, in
dress and manner, is one of the means he uses to
fend off the world, avoid participation in it. . . .
Nixon restored the white-tie ceremony to the White
House. Some, it is true, took the toy hats and tunics
added to White House police as a sign of Nixon's
imagination. . . . Quite the opposite. Each added
symbol of uniform, function, office makes man's role
in the social chess game clearer, his place marked,
moves limited. Clothes structure a situation.—GARY
WILLS, Nixon Agonistes**

A performer on stage or in public wants to impress an audience with a special image of his character. Like any good performer, de Gaulle knew how to dress for the occasion. TV changes the nature of performance. All the TV images—a space flight or a soap opera—have the same visual *weight*. The television tube puts every viewer in the front row, center. We scrutinize faces at closer range, and without the depth of three-dimensional space we cannot see the performance in the perspective of its entire environment. The TV "set" is too small. The close-up forces the performer to be even more careful about how he looks and how he "comes across."

PRESIDENTIAL ACTING STYLE. "The success of any TV performer depends on his achievement of a low-pressure style of presentation." McLuhan has written. The harder a man tries, the better he must hide it. The television demands gentle wit, irony, understatement: the quality of Eugene McCarthy. The TV politician cannot make a speech: he must engage in intimate conversation. He must never press. He should suggest, not state; request not demand. Nonchalance is the key word. Carefully studied nonchalance. Warmth and sincerity are desirable but must be handled with care. Unfiltered, they may be fatal. Television did great harm to Hubert Humphrey. His excesses—talking too long and too fervently, which were merely annoying in an auditorium, became lethal in a television studio.—The Selling of the President, 1968

The low-definition of the television image and the distance of the audience from the actual event make it hard for the viewer to understand or accept artifice in a "live performance." On stage, we assume a person will be "made-up"; the intimacy of the TV set implies personality which exists without *façade*. But, on TV, the make-up is there; it is simply not noticeable. At a play, "magic" is believing through the acceptance of artifice; we assume TV is "real" and believe it is through the tacit denial of artifice. And yet, as a breakdown of President Nixon's TV "appearances" illustrates, his speeches on television are carefully managed performances, where the message is not just in the words. He is acting out a Presidential-leadership role; and his impact is *staged*: his gestures are clearly a dramatic illusion of his intentions. He is a star performer, and everything is controlled to highlight his performance.

★ ★ ★ ★ ★ ★ ★ ★ ★ ★ ★ ★ ★ ★ ★ ★ ★ ★

THE RICHARD NIXON SHOW

★ ★ ★ ★ ★ ★ ★ ★ ★ ★ ★ ★ ★ ★ ★ ★ ★

The Look

A. He looks good on his feet and shooting "in the round" gives dimension to him.

B. Standing adds to his "feel" of confidence and the viewers' "feel" of his confidence.

C. He still uses his arms a little too "predictably" and a little too often, but at this point it is better not to inhibit him.

D. He seems to be comfortable on his feet and even appears graceful and relaxed. . . .

E. His eye contact is good with the panelists, but he should play a little more to the home audience via the head-on camera. I would like to talk to him about this.

F. We are still working on lightening up his eyes a bit, but this is not a major problem. This will be somewhat tougher in smaller studios, but don't worry, he will never look bad.

1. I may lower the front two key spots a bit.
2. I may try slightly whiter make-up on upper eyelids.
3. I may lower the riser he stands on a couple of inches.

G. The "arena" effect is excellent and he plays to all areas well. The look has "guts". . . .

J. Generally, he has a very "Presidential" look and style—he smiles easily (and looks good doing it). He should continue to make lighter comments once in a while for pacing.

Staging

A. The microphone cord needs to be dressed and looped to the side.

B. Bud Wilkinson felt there should be more women on the panel since over half the voters are women. Maybe combine a category i.e., woman reporter or Negro woman. . . .

E. The family should be in the audience at every show. —The Selling of the President, 1968

Nixon plays *to win* an election, just as a stage performer *competes* for an audience's attention and approval. Combat is part of the thrill and danger of public performances. Technique keeps the chinks in emotional armor from showing.

Even in the "battle of the sexes" men "dress up" and women "put on a face"—a ritual readying where the armor of clothes and cosmetics is both an offensive and defensive weapon. It is not without significance that Alexander Pope's *The Rape of the Lock* describes Belinda making herself up in front of a mirror in a military, mock-heroic tone.

Now awful Beauty puts on all its Arms;
The Fair each moment rises in her Charms,
Repairs her Smiles, awakens ev'ry Grace,
And calls forth all the Wonders of her Face;
Sees by Degrees a purer Blush arise,
And keener Lightnings quicken in her eyes.

In reinventing an idea of herself, Belinda, like all performers, becomes her own hero. The *persona* is dramatically real and alluring. Beauty, Pope illustrates, is a conjuring trick which gives the appearance of perfection. We use the same words to describe Beauty's mercurial perfection as we do a stage performance: "breathtaking," "spellbinding," "captivating." The words indicate a suspension of disbelief, a fiction which captures the viewer's imagination and forces acceptance of the other's identity. The effect and intention of a successful *persona* are the same: a conscious act of *re-creation*.

THE MASK OF DRESS. Even if each woman dresses in conformity with her status, a game is still being played. . . . It is not only that girdle, brassiere, hair-dye, make-up disguise the body and face; but that the least sophisticated woman, once she is "dressed," does not present herself to observation; she is, like the picture or the statue or the actor on the stage, an agent through whom is suggested someone not there—that is, the character she represents, but is not. It is this identification with something unreal, fixed, perfect as the hero of a novel, as a portrait or a bust, that gratifies her; she strives to identify herself with this figure and thus to seem to herself to be stabilized, justified in her splendor. . . . —SIMONE DE BEAUVOIR, The Second Sex

Not every actor is right for the same part. Most roles can be "learned," but effective characterization comes out of emotions and instincts which are discovered easily by the actor, then pursued and refined. We cast ourselves, usually, in parts where we can best succeed. Belinda is a "knockout," she dominates her scene. Her role gives her the flamboyance and confidence to be free. She uses her *persona* as easily as she plays cards. Other women might refuse to play her kind of game or might fail at it. Significantly, they would be faulted in theatrical terms for "not doing more with themselves." But, as Simone de Beauvoir points out, both sexes paint a picture of themselves, a representation which approximates who they think they are or would like to be. C. G. Jung argues that role-playing is the necessary fluid through which the individual flows into society. Roles are shaped and developed through social demands. On stage and in life, the discovery and acting out of roles is an attempt to impose an order on the world.

SOCIETY AS AUDIENCE. Society expects, and indeed must expect, every individual to play the part assigned to him as perfectly as possible, so that a man who is a parson . . . must at all times . . . play the role of a parson in a flawless manner. Society demands this as a kind of surety: each must stand at his post, here a cobbler, there a poet. No man is expected to be both . . . that would be "queer." Such a man would be "different" from other people, not quite reliable. In the academic world he would be a dilettante, in politics an unpredictable quantity, in religion a free thinker—in short he would always be suspected of unreliability and incompetence, because society is persuaded that only the cobbler who is not a poet can provide workmanlike shoes.—C. G. JUNG, Two Essays on Analytic Psychology

This social pressure can lead to strained, confused and disastrous social performances. Willy Loman in Arthur Miller's *Death of a Salesman* and Nora in Ibsen's *A Doll's House* are victims, unable to fulfill the demands of their roles and trapped in somebody else's dream for them. Yet they, like us, carry on. We are creatures of play which we can turn either to escape or, as does Nora in the final moments of *A Doll's House*, to discovery.

Courtship is one of the many public scenes where impersonation is most conspicuously the proper style of performance. The history of stage literature is dominated by man's theatrical disguises in love. We "accentuate the positive." We "*play* hard to get." Even when we idealize these moments as the most vivid in our emotional life, their clarity stems from their powerful artifice, by which feeling is at first hidden and then channeled into an exquisite intimacy. All caveats of How To Love, How To Dress, How To Get Your Man are unabashed exercises in heightening the masquerade which is courtship.

STAGING YOURSELF. . . . Be yourself, but be an improved you. Invest in contact lenses. Have your nose fixed, your ears pinned back, or your teeth capped. Get professional advice about cosmetics and clothes. If you're not very pretty, be well-read. If you're not intellectual or pretty, be athletic, charming and charitable. Build yourself some assets. . . . . Get a prop. Bike ride. Fly a kite. Buy a dog, and walk it. Dog Hill in Central Park is a great place to meet all kinds of people.—STANLEE MILLER COY, The Single Girl's Book

As any actor knows, the right prop and the right costume often suggest, even compel, an energy and a performance that one could not achieve without them. The stage actor is seducing an audience the way lovers tempt each other in life. Impersonation is a means of coping with the terror of identity and of genuine freedom. Jean-Paul Sartre has written: "The Beloved is a look." By presenting oneself in a certain way, the lover recreates himself into a fascinating object for the observation of his audience/partner.

SEDUCTION SCENES. To seduce is to risk assuming my object-state completely for the Other; it is to put myself beneath his look and to make him look at me; it is to risk the danger of being seen in order to effect a new departure and to appropriate the Other in and by means of my object-ness.— JEAN-PAUL SARTRE, Being and Nothingness

In every seduction, sight, sound, smell, set are manipulated to sustain the fantasy of the impersonation. Eroticism is the art of suggestion: the hint of submission or domination.

WHAT MAKES A SEXY ROOM? Lighting is the most important. The room should be neither dark nor brightly lit, but somewhere in between . . . The best lighting is indirect. Use warm-toned incandescent bulbs such as readily available pink ones, for they give the skin a glowing quality. Don't use any blue or so-called daylight bulbs. They bleach color from the skin, making people look like animated corpses rather than glowing lovers. . . . Fragrance also enriches the atmosphere of a room. . . . Stick incense, tall and delicately thin, is least expensive and looks the most dramatic while burning.—LOCKE MC CORKLE, How To Make Love

Fantasy plays an important part in seduction. Emotions become real through the performance itself. Courtship is galvanized by the theatrical exhibition of lovers' impersonations, but this dramatic display and ritual posing are not limited to *homo sapiens*.

ANIMAL ARTIFICE. Fully matured ganders advertise their love by all the means at their disposal, and it is really quite amazing what changes can be wrought in the outer appearance of a bird lacking special organs of display. A fish can make its colors glow in sudden iridescence, it can unfold its fins, a peacock can raise and rustle his wonderful tail coverts, a man can dress up in his best clothes in order to appear as different as possible from his common everyday self. A gander can do none of these things, and yet it has happened to me that I simply failed to recognize a well-known individual after he had fallen in love. The tension of all muscles is increased, which gives the bird a curious stance of pride and alertness and changes the contours of his body considerably. Every single movement, walking, swimming, and flying, even preening or turning his head, is performed with an excessive expenditure of energy.—KONRAD LORENZ, On Aggression

Even in masturbation, with the erotic partner absent, the practitioner impersonates the fantasy figure, a ventriloquist dramatizing the silent conquest, the drama of costume and gesture radiated in the artifice of courtship.

IMPERSONATION. . . . I once cored an apple, saw to my astonishment (and with the aid of my obsession) what it looked like, and ran off into the woods to fall upon the orifice of the fruit, pretending that the cool and mealy hole was actually between the legs of that mythical being who always called me Big Boy when she pleaded for what no girl in all recorded history had ever had. "Oh shove it in me, Big Boy" cried the cored apple that I banged silly on that picnic. "Big Boy, Big Boy, oh give me all you've got," begged the empty milk bottle that I kept hidden in our storage basement, to drive wild after school with my vaselined upright. . . .—PHILIP ROTH, Portnoy's Complaint

Sexual perversion merely exaggerates the theatrical, exotic displays of everyman. Conventional courtship is a comparatively mild game of slap and tickle. The thrill and danger of the transaction lies in the surrender *and* renewal of human freedom. In sadomasochistic spectacles, impersonation is carried to elaborate extremes: freedom is a dramatized slavery.

It is significant that the Marquis de Sade, whose name and sexual practices added a clinical term to the vocabulary, was a failed but prolific playwright who staged his own, more successful fantasies of bondage in life. Fantastic sets, masks, and costumes added to the elaborate titillation of de Sade's scenarios of debauchery. In his specific outlines (almost neoclassic in their ordered routines for bacchanalia) the theatricality and suggestion of environment and masquerade added to the frenzy of passion.

THE MARQUIS' SCENES. . . . A bascule carrries her down into a small crypt hung in black and furnished with a prie-dieu, a coffin, and an assortment of death's heads. She sees six specters armed with clubs, swords, pistols, sabers, poignards, and lances, and each is about to pierce her in a different place. Overcome by fear, she sways, is about to fall; the man enters, catches her in his arms, and flogs her until he is weary, then he discharges as he embuggers her. If she is unconscious at the time he enters, and this is frequently the case, his lash restores her to her senses.

. . . He slips a noose around the whore's throat and hangs her. Her feet rest upon a stool, a cord is tied to one leg of the stool, he sits in an armchair, watching and having the whore's daughter frig him. . . .
—One Hundred Twenty Days of Sodom

The sexual thrill lies in the fantasy of total domination being acted out, the manipulation of environment and personality into a full-blooded spectacle of desire. "What does a successful playwright or actor do?" asks Geoffrey Gorer, commenting on de Sade's theater of perversion.

By his skills, he commands the emotions of his audience, makes them laugh or cry, shudder or exult as he plans; he produces visible and audible changes in the people who are under his spell. But in a crude and concrete way, this is precisely what a sadist wishes to do to his victims; in a greater number of cases one might well say the sadist is acting out a play with an audience of one.
—*The Life and Ideas of the Marquis de Sade*

The famous Hell-Fire caves in eighteenth-century England also made a theatrical spectacle of profanation. With their black masses, their whores dressed as nuns and wearing masks, the practitioners could lose their identity and acquire the symbolic power of gods. (Significantly, the man who founded the infamous club, Sir Francis Dashwood, was referred to as "Lord Le Dispenser".) Describing the masquerades and ritual wardrobes of the bacchantes, Ronald Fuller's *Hell-Fire Francis* emphasizes that "They would all have been entirely happy and at home on the variety stage, in a kind of permanent pantomime touring the provinces. Only in the theatre could their passion for posing and dressing up have been gratified."

Carried to its extreme, impersonation denies all sense of individuality and allows the performer to gloss-over self-loathing and glory in his inauthenticity. He revels in a spectacle of his void. Jean Genet's *The Balcony*, set in a whorehouse that caters to these erotic/theatrical fantasies, dramatizes the disguises, the surreal acting out of roles. Once a role is assumed, certain emotions are necessary to fulfill its function. A whore plays a thief facing the judgment of an Executioner and a Judge who are paying for the privilege of their impersonation.

THE EXECUTIONER: *I mean the confession is supposed to come later. Plead not guilty.*
THE THIEF: *What, and get beaten again!*
THE JUDGE (mealy-mouthed): *Exactly my child: and get beaten. You must first deny, then admit and repent. I want to see hot tears gush from your lovely eyes. Oh! I want you to be drenched in them. The power of tears! . . . Where's my statute-book?* (He fishes under his robe and pulls out a book)
THE THIEF: *I've already cried.*
THE JUDGE (he seems to be reading): *Under the blows. I want tears of repentance. When I see you wet as a meadow I'll be utterly satisfied!*

At the finale, Genet emphasizes that all our functions are masks: impersonations through which we impose pain and conflict on others in order to gratify a contrived self-image. Irma, the madam, turns out the lights.

In a little while, I'll have to start all over again . . . put all the lights on again . . . dress up. . . . (A cock crows) *Dress up . . . ah, the disguises! Distribute roles again . . . assume my own. . . .* (She stops in the middle of the stage, facing the audience) *. . . Prepare yours . . . judges, generals, bishops, chamberlains, rebels who allow the revolt to congeal, I'm going to prepare my costumes and studios for tomorrow. . . . You must now go home, where everything—you can be quite sure—will be falser than here. . . .*

In daily life, we are conscious of "keeping *up* appearances," "making a good *impression*." Even if we do not think of ourselves as performers, we are still "cast" in "roles" in our various domestic "scenes." Society demands

a certain kind of performance. Etiquette is an institutionalized "routine" for proper behavior, a system which
teaches us how "to act" in different situations. Here, as in
every production, style of dress, of gesture, of language, of
setting must fit the needs of the situation. The goal is to
be acceptable. Each individual wants to *imitate* the ideal
of the gentleman or lady. This is an act of impersonation.
Amy Vanderbilt's *Complete Book of Etiquette* sets down
the background for this performance. As on stage, appearance must be matched with energy; the role must be played
with conviction.

Good manners and appropriate dress are, or should be,
part and parcel of gentle people. Notice the word "appropri-
ate." Clothing need not be expensive or of the finest
needlework or tailoring, but it must suit the occasion on
which it is worn. We are not born with the knowledge
that French heels are in poor taste with a classic tweed suit,
that boisterousness is out of place in church. Precept
and example show us how ladies and gentlemen should
look and act. And feel. Outward conformity to a code is
never enough. . . . Good manners have to do with the
emotions. To make them ring true, one must feel them, not
merely exhibit them.

Just as we appreciate a stage actor who performs so
"naturally" we don't think he's "acting," so, also, does the
well-mannered life-performer want his impersonation to
go unnoticed, to *seem* natural. The instinct in life, as on
stage, is to act out an idea that you want seen, "to feel it,
not just exhibit it." Hiding an emotional truth or an intimacy which might betray the characterization is a crucial
tension to this kind of playing. Etiquette emphasizes artifice and disguise. Emily Post stresses this aspect of public
acting:

Begin by shunning conspicuous manners and conspicuous
clothes. . . . Do not expose your private affairs, feelings
or innermost thoughts in public. You are knocking down
the walls of your house when you do. . . .

Etiquette ritualizes suppression. As public performers,
we watch what we say and how we say it, calibrating our
delivery to the specific demands of the audience. We are
both in a role and outside it, judging our actions. We with-
draw that part of our real feeling which would jeopardize
the credibility of our role or our acceptance. Etiquette is
an exercise in emotional withdrawal, a code that stresses
putting your best foot forward so as not to make a *faux pas*
(false step). This *dis-simulation* is a performance. It is a
re-action, a means of filtering human energy and creating
a psychic invisibility. A *"some-body"* acts like "every-body"

should; symbolically assuming the position of a *"no-body."*

Octavio Paz, the Mexican poet, has observed: "Dissimulation requires greater subtlety; the person who dissimulates is not counterfeiting, but attempting to become invisible, to pass unnoticed without renouncing individuality." Emily Post would agree that this was the function of manners; but Paz's provocative contention glosses over two facts. First, the choice of making yourself emotionally/morally invisible is itself an invention, an imitation of Nothingness. Second, individuality is an ideal whose root meaning implies *not* separation from a group *but* inseparability. If we act "invisible," we deny authentic relations with others. Carried to its extreme, dissimulation separates us from our self. Whether Uriah Heep or an Uncle Tom, when etiquette is confused with identity, the person has lost touch with real emotion and authentic selfhood. Suppression, which may be socially necessary, gives way to repression—a withdrawal of attention so that the thought, feeling, event which is to be repressed is at last expelled from consciousness, and we are unable to recall it. The true self is forgotten; the person is a shell of disguises. There is no spontaneity, concentration, or creative thrust to his actions.

A false self may be worn by a person, or even a culture. False roles have a powerful personal and social effect. Codes of public behavior become performances in which pain, vulnerability, and often truth can be hidden. As psychiatrist Frieda Fordham has observed:

There is always the danger of identifying oneself with the role one fills, a danger that is not obvious when the role is a good one and fits the person well. . . . Perhaps some crisis will occur which calls for flexibility or a completely new way of reacting, or a human situation may be reached where the lack of a genuinely individual emotional response spells tragedy.

Stanislavski reminded his actors that in assuming a role they must not lose contact with themselves; the same is true of a culture. A society, like a performer, can become frozen in public postures.

For decades, America has put up a convincing dramatic and legal show by which it convinces itself of its authentic founding spirit and its continued integrity as a young nation. "The New Deal," "The New Frontier," "The Great Society" are shibboleths keyed to the future, not the past. While the society goes forward, it has failed in some deep spiritual sense to comprehend the genocide of the Indians, the oppression of the Blacks, the stalled mobility of the poor. The lack of a cultural memory is its most notorious symptom, the aftereffects of generations of bogus social impersonations. To a large section of the American establishment, their oppressiveness is not credible since it is not visible. The scenario of their existence, the style in which they perform and which they demand from others whom they meet keeps them from facing the sins they commit and have committed in the name of life, liberty, and the pursuit of happiness. Etiquette keeps the dream of their role intact and the problems comparatively invisible. The gut response to protest is on the level of manners. Protest seems to them rude, vulgar, disgusting. It's not the way gentlemen settle things. Manners, on this level, seek to keep failure out of sight and out of earshot.

Minority protest is a reaction to enforced invisibility. The rage, schizoid and often suicidal impulses come from trying to break out of the theatrical double-bind that they are forced to act out. "Uncle Toming," for instance, is a performance where both the white society and the Negro acting the role are confirmed in race "inferiority." The Black man is conscious of being at once present and "not there": a condition reflected in such Black literature as *The Invisible Man* and *Nobody Knows My Name*. To act "invisible" puts Blacks or any other minority victim in an untenable position, one which is maintained through economic authority and rigid environmental pressures. R. D. Laing describes this theatrical routine which leads to comparable melodramatic means of fending it off:

THE DOUBLE-BIND VAUDEVILLE. In an untenable position, no matter how he feels or how he acts, or what meaning the situation has, his feelings are denuded of validity, his acts are stripped of their motives, intentions, and consequences, the situation is robbed of its meaning. This may be done unintentionally, as a by-product of each person's self-deception. Those who deceive themselves are obliged to deceive others. It is impossible for me to maintain a false picture of myself unless I falsify your picture of yourself and of me. I must disparage you if you are genuine, accuse you of being a phoney when you comply with what I want, say you are selfish if you go your own way, ridicule you for being immature if you try to be unselfish, and so on. The person caught within such a muddle does not know whether he is coming or going. In these circumstances what we call psychosis may be a desperate effort to hold on to something. It is not surprising that the something may be what we call "delusions."—R. D. LAING, The Self and Other

---

Often, no matter how self-conscious we are, we expose emotions and drop our masks. We say we "let our hair down." At these moments, we are not "composed"; we are vulnerable. But, in front of certain "invisible" people (servants, waiters, cab-drivers), we feel neither fear nor guilt. Telyeghin, a landowner reduced to poverty in Anton Chekhov's *Uncle Vanya*, sits quietly amid the dreary embarrassment of Vanya's family squabbles. When he speaks up, it is to remind them of his name!

TELYEGHIN: *Excuse me. My name's not Ivan Ivanovich, it's Ilya Ilyich . . . Ilya Ilyich Telyeghin or as some people call me on account of my spotty face, Waffles. I'm Soniechka's godfather and his Excellency, your husband, knows me very well. I'm now living here on your estate. . . . You may have been so kind to notice that I have dinner with you every day.*

On stage, Chekhov creates a character who is a living apparition. Essentially, Telyeghin is a companion, a role bridging functions of both servant and friend. The servant's function is to be unnoticeable but "on call," he is not a felt *presence*. Emily Post describes the performance required of servants. "The *well-trained* servant is faultlessly neat in appearance, reticent in manner, speaks in a low voice, and moves silently." They are responsible for recognizing others, but also *for being unrecognizable*. The same applies to the military, where the "enlisted man" is told to "speak when spoken to," "look sharp," and "salute anything that moves." Regulations prevent the soldier from "talking back" to his superiors. The military judges solely by appearance: required response and attitude is indicated by costume (uniform). Medals, insignia, and bars indicate without words an officer's military history and his "position" (rank). Officers stand out, both visually and physically. They are always dramatically set apart from the enlisted man. The soldier's goal in such a tightly structured society is to "fit in," not to "act up." He is a number and a name:

in the military set-up, he is a nobody and success is measured by how well the soldier "plays the game." This institutionalized "invisibility" is a psychological necessity for military control. Identity is redefined through military values; the ordinary soldier is rewarded for how efficiently he functions as a cog in the war machine. The violence, boredom, and chaos of military life demand this ritual performance from the soldiers, not only as acts of continual subjugation of will but of reaffirmation of military goals. If things are "looking good," the assumption is that they must *be* good. The soldier, like the servant, accepts this invisibility because of the threat of power and his own animal impulse to survive. The ghetto and the reservation are collective extensions of this imposed individual invisibility.

GHOST TOWNS. Our ideas about institutionalizing the aged, psychotic, retarded and infirm are based on a pattern of thought that we might call the Toilet Assumption—the notion that unwanted matter, unwanted difficulties, unwanted complexities and obstacles will disappear if they are removed from our immediate field of vision. . . . Our approach to social problems is to decrease their visibility: out of sight, out of mind. This is the real foundation of racial segregation, especially its most extreme case, the Indian "reservation."—PHILIP SLATER, The Pursuit of Loneliness

But this kind of performance does not have to be institutionalized to be real. Do we see garbage collectors, doormen, drunks? Often, they stage performances—heads down, bodies slumped, clothes tattered and *un-attractive*—which signal their own sense of worthlessness. They want to be invisible: they know they are "eyesores." Their whole productions says: "Pretend I never happened." Beggars, often turn this performance into profit. They force people to take notice of their condition of invisibility. People give money to "get rid of them."

The master-slave relationship as outlined by Karl Marx is a reaction to the destructive economic scenes being played out on workers which force them to impersonate nonbeings: becoming mere commodities in order to survive. The boss-worker, the donor-beggar, the officer-enlisted man are all relationships requiring performances in which one man's freedom is defined by the destruction of another's.

MARX AND IMITATION. A being only considers himself independent when he owes his existence to himself as a dependent being. But if I live completely by the grace of another I owe him not only the sustenance of my life, but if he has, moreover, created my life—if he is the source of my life, and if it is not of my own creation, my life has necessarily a course of this kind outside it.—Philosophical Manuscripts

"Alienation" is the condition of being forced to exist at a distance from yourself. Feelings, ideas, and individuality are squashed because they are not useful to the master's plan or enterprise.

Women's Liberation is one of many contemporary examples of the passion to break down master-slave impersonations: to put women in touch with their real emotions and desires by stripping away the inauthentic performances demanded of them as housewives and as members of the "second sex." The drudge, the spender, the chief cook and bottlewasher, the sex object are roles which women conventionally accept but which, to many, are unfulfilling. Taught to believe that "a woman's place is in the home," the wife acts out her role convincingly; but it does not always gratify her or help her to grow. Like so many impersonations, the masquerade may succeed in gaining approval from others, while eroding the spiritual life of the actor.

Like a student so busy showing he is paying attention that he does not hear what is being said, the impersonation of acceptable identities may put real identity out of reach. Bad roles are not necessarily the result of bad impersonation. The "freak," the "beat," the "revolutionary" are exaggerated reactions to conventional roles. Even here, the performance becomes shallow, and mistakes sincerity for understanding and determination for depth. The promise of vitality may yield more curiosity than conviction. Style is the quickest revolution. It is easier to change your appearance than to change the society and the self.

There is another kind of acting which does not want to impersonate but to transcend, which does not seek to disguise failure but acknowledges it in performance. This acting is not a process of *hiding*, but *being*. We know it in the fine frenzy of the clowns—Charlie Chaplin, Buster Keaton, the Marx Brothers, Bert Lahr, Bobby Clark— as well as in the more systematized aesthetic of Jerzy Grotowski's Polish Lab Theatre. Here, the performer goes to physical excess. "Men have always expressed their deepest joys, fears, and longings in acts, shouts, jumps, gestures, and struts" (Harvey Cox, *The Feast of Fools*). The clowns turn their performance into an ecstasy of movement and metaphor, a unique signature of their inner lives. Personality and emotion are made visible through the body; gestures, in their outrageousness, assume an exaggerated dream quality. By going to extremes, the performer tests his being and moves himself closer to an intimate unity between body and spirit. On stage, he accomplishes a clarity and sense of renewal that elude him in daily life. With an audience as medium, the performer is transported beyond his ordinary potential. We say the great clowns are "inspired." Our language correctly implies a connection between spirituality and performance.

JERZY GROTOWSKI. At a moment of psychic shock, a moment of terror, of mortal danger, or tremendous joy, a man does not behave "naturally." A man in an elevated spiritual state uses rhythmically articulated signs, begins to dance, to sing.—Towards a Poor Theatre

---

J. M. SYNGE. When people are in pain themselves, they make no attempt to hide or control their feelings. An old man who was ill in the winter took me out the other day to show me how far down the road they could hear him yelling "the time he had a pain in his head."—The Aran Islands

---

Our language shows us just how far we are "transported." We say: "I was *beside* myself," "I nearly jumped out of my skin," "I lost control of myself," "I freaked-*out*," "I blew my mind." In all these idioms, there is a sense of action being carried to the extreme, the spirit escaping or being wrenched from its "normal" container. An ecstatic performance is scary: it mingles joy and sorrow, life and death, logic and irrational inspiration, the human and the animal. It breaks boundaries and redefines freedom. And yet it is precisely this quality of being *seized*, of inhabiting not another's role but the fullness of one's own moment that is the most riveting, upsetting, and dignified of dramatic acts. The risk in this performance makes it dangerous; the revelation gives it nobility.

The clown transforms into art the ecstatic ritual performances shared by all civilizations through the ages. Even if the modern audiences sit sedentary in their seats, the clowns can make them—they say—"hysterical," a condition which intimates, if it does not fulfill, the nature of mass hysteria once channeled spontaneously into ancient Dionysian rites. "Ritual dances provide a religious experience that seems more satisfying and convincing than any other," wrote Aldous Huxley. "It is with their muscles that they most easily obtain knowledge of the Divine."

The clowns are open to the suggestion of their bodies and the will of the audience. They are free, galvanized by a spirit that inspires them to incredible physical accomplishments. Like the Dionysiac dancing cults described in the

Bacchae (that self-surrender which once begun is difficult to stop), the audience witnesses the power of this possession: an idea seized by and penetrating through the performer's being. While the clowns are not shamans—inspired priests in touch with the spirit world for whom they minister on earth—they can "heal" an audience with laughter or transport its imagination to a heightened clarity about human existence. The culture treats the greatest of them as symbolic priests: figures, at least of reverence and reflection. The "magic" of the clown's stage performance has interesting correlations and limitations compared with tribal rituals.

THE SHAMAN AND THE TRIBAL RITE. The rhythmic music and singing, and later the dancing of the shaman, gradually involve every participant more and more in a collective action. When the audience begins to repeat the refrains together with the assistants, only those who are defective fail to join the chorus. The tempo of the action increases, the shaman with a spirit is no more an ordinary man or relative, but is "placing" (i.e., incarnation) of the spirit; the spirit acts together with the audience and this is felt by everyone. The state of many participants is now near to that of the shaman himself, and only a strong belief that when the shaman is there the spirit may only enter him, restrains the participants from being possessed in mass by the spirit. This is a very important condition of shamanizing which does not however reduce mass susceptibility to the suggestion, hallucinations, and unconscious acts produced in a state of mass ecstasy. When the shaman feels that the audience is with him and follows him he becomes still more active and this effect is transmitted to his audience. After shamanizing, the audience recollects various moments of the performance, their great psychosociological emotion and the hallucinations of sights and hearing which they have experienced. They then have a deep satisfaction—much greater than that from emotions produced by theatrical or musical performancess, literature and general artistic phenomena of the European complex, because in shamanizing the audience at the same time acts and participates.—S. M. SHIROKOGOROFF, Psychomental Complex of the Tungus

On stage, the outrageous performances of the clowns affect an audience as a hallucination. Objects are seen anew; a private language often is spoken and makes sense. Masks fall away and human vulnerability is on display. The clowns may have taken many "roles," but their success was in *"being* themselves." Keaton is always Keaton, Groucho always Groucho, no matter how they are disguised. It is no accident that these men are the central figures of American theater and are resonant symbols of the society's mythology. In their acrobatic *élan*, they opened themselves up; their gestures were "inspired" and their exaggeration discovered and incarnated the emotional

dilemmas of the time. Their private failures—ugliness, ignorance, clumsiness, rage, inarticulateness—were made public and turned to hilarious victories on stage. They actualized their inner life. They expressed with every part of their body. Singing, dancing, tumbling, leaping, mugging—they did not imitate the details of everyday life; they *transcended* them.

The clowns turned their disciplined bodies into an intimate expression of individual energy. The clowns never explained themselves, but their bodies gave off many silent messages. They simply existed in front of an audience. The more honest (and painful) the statement of their gestures, the more shocking and hilarious to the audience. In their ecstatic groping, egged on by the audience, feeling out new ideas in the flesh, they uncovered the fullness of their comic identity.

BERT LAHR. One day I went "gnong, gnong, gnong." I don't know why. I just discovered it. It seemed right. The audience laughed, so I kept it in.

The clowns were in perpetual motion; their stage performances were a visible, real liberation. On stage, they dramatized their profoundest yearnings and found a means of fulfilling them in action. Their comedy—so intimately connected with their entire human mechanism—was specific and elusive: a riddle which surprised and fascinated the spectator.

NORMAN O. BROWN. Enigmatic form is living form; like life, an iridescence; an invitation to dance; a temptation; or irritation. No satisfying solutions; nothing to rest in; nothing to weigh us down.— Love's Body

With the clowns, nothing could be taken for granted; every object and posture could change shape in the energy of each comic moment. The stage was dangerous because the comics were free. Their openness and anarchy meant that the stage could be as unpredictable as life itself. "Anything could happen." What Antonin Artaud says of the Balinese theater also pertains to the American stage clowns: ". . . through the labyrinth of their gestures, attitudes and sudden cries, through the gyrations and turns which leave no portion of the stage space unutilized, the sense of a new physical language, based upon signs and no longer upon

words, is liberated." Of course, clowns told jokes; but their
appeal was in the quality of their being. Clowning energy
took on superhuman dimensions: the bounds of rationality
had been transcended. Laughter at their delirium on stage
was a purifying act; for, as Artaud saw, when the stage
shares the delirium, it "impels men to see themselves as they
are, it causes the mask to fall, reveals the lie, the slackness,
baseness, and hypocrisy of the world. . . ." Our terms for
their performance "insane," "crazy," "bedlam," "mayhem"
show how far the clowns departed from the rational norm.
The great clowns dealt with and went beyond the culture.

ARTAUD ON THE MARX BROTHERS. The contemporary theatre is decadent because it has lost the feeling on the one hand for seriousness and on the other for laughter; because it has broken away from gravity, from the effects that are immediate and painful—in a word from Danger. . . . In Animal Crackers . . . it is only at the end that things grow complicated, that objects, animals, sounds, master and servants, hosts and guests, everything goes mad, runs wild, and revolts amid the simultaneously ecstatic and lucid comments of one of the Marx Brothers, inspired by the spirit he has finally been able to unleash and whose stupefied momentary commentator he seems to be. There is nothing at once so hallucinatory and so terrible as this type of man-hunt, this battle of rivals, this chase in the shadows of a cow barn, a stable draped in cobwebs, while men, women and animals break their bounds and land in the middle of a heap of crazy objects, each whose movement or noise functions in its turn.—Theatre and Its Double

---

New theater seeks to systematize many of the physical
and emotional results best exemplified in the clowns. It
wants a protean performance in which the actor's growth
is visible, in which through discipline an idea can be seen
to emerge through the body. In this kind of performance,
mystery is locked into the elaborate, personal choreography
of gesture and the idiosyncratic vocal sounds emitted to
match the performers spiritual state. There is no intention
to imitate the real world, but to find a performing style
and a language which has the mystery and challenge of
authentic play. In this style, the performer accomplishes
an "exemplary action," a physical feat which, like watching

a great ballplayer, inspires wonder and deep respect for the nature of his effort. This type of theater answers deep psychic needs in our contemporary life-performance.

GROTOWSKI AND THE PROTEAN PERFORM- ANCE. Theatre—through the actor's technique, his art in which the living organism strives for higher motives—provides an opportunity for what could be called integration, the discarding of masks, the revealing of the real substance; a totality of phys-

ical and mental reactions. . . . Here we can see the theatre's therapeutic function for people in our present-day civilization. It is true that the actor accomplishes this act, but he can only do so through an encounter with the spectator—intimately, visibly, not hiding behind a cameraman, wardrobe mis- tress, stage designer, or make-up girl—in direct con- frontation with him and somehow instead of him. The actor's act—discarding half-measures, reveal- ing, opening up, emerging from himself as opposed to closing up—is an invitation to the spectator. This act could be compared to an act of the most deeply rooted, genuine love between two human beings— this is just a comparison since we can only refer to this "emergence from oneself" through analogy. This act, paradoxical and borderline, we call a total act. In our opinion it epitomizes the actor's deepest calling.—Towards a Poor Theater

This type of performance displays and develops a protean theatrical style. On stage, the body is freed to express itself in the fullness of its symbol-giving potential. "It means that the actor will never possess a permanently 'closed' technique, for at each stage of his self-scrutiny, each challenge, each *excess*, each breaking down hidden barriers, he will encounter new theatrical problems on a higher level" (Grotowski). This kind of stage performance, defining man in continual motion and transformation, incarnates transcendence. The "meaning" is in the stage of the actor's *being*. Excess yields insight. This protean stage performance parallels the contemporary protean life-performance, a style that psychiatrist Robert J. Lifton has characterized as "an interminable series of experiments and explorations, some shallow, some profound, each of which can be readily abandoned in favor of still new, psychological quests" (*Boundaries*). On stage and in life, freedom is exhibited through struggle. Our language gives us clues to our protean life performances. We "put ourselves through *changes*," "let it all hang out," "do our own thing." These acts in life are extreme, dangerous, and revealing.

MOVEMENT AS MEANING. Meaning is not in things but in between; in the iridescence, the interplay; in the interconnections. . . . Meaning is transitional as it is transitory.—NORMAN O. BROWN

Just as the limitation of the protean performance on stage is acrobatics, the limitation of the protean life style is mere plasticity. But, at its deepest level, both kinds of protean performances indicate an existential, even sacrificial quality to living. New terms in our language—"sensory awareness" "consciousness-raising," "getting it together"— hint at this quality of change, the impulse to go deeper while being at once more open and in more complete control of one's own "form." In the protean life performance, the actor is working to accomplish the full awareness of his moment and his evolution in it. Claude Brown wrote in *Esquire*:

Soul is bein' true to yourself, to what is you. Now hold on: soul is . . . that . . . uninhibited . . . no extremely uninhibited self . . . expression that goes into practically every Negro endeavor. That's soul. And there's swagger in it, man. It's exhibitionism, and it's effortless. Effortless. You don't need to put it on; it just comes out.

On stage, in the protean performance, the actor is deepened with each new physical discovery and symbolically reborn. (After each pratfall, the clown bounces back.) "The actor must accomplish an act of the soul" (Grotowski). To do this, the stage performer must sacrifice his spirit in order to find it. The ritual *excess* of energy is an act of renewal. In life, we have many less artful but no less real protean performances. "The fiesta," writes Octavio Paz, "is not only an *excess*, a ritual squandering . . . it is also a revolt, a sudden immersion in the formless, in pure being" (*The Labyrinth of Solitude*). In America, we have few authentic public ceremonies where form is tested. The protean impulse—for the body and the mind to change shape, for life to expand through excess and experiment— parallels the yearning for rebirth in the experience. Intensity, discovery, liberation, psychic death/rebirth are being *lived through*. The jolts and spasms of protean transformation—in Grotowski's theater or in the psychedelic experience—are attempts to shatter the masks which hide being. They typify the internal protean battle: "to beat oneself into [new] shape." Even in our natural daily life, the extravagant rhythms and movement of sexual intercourse are a protean performance. As Alan Harrington has pointed out, sex "is a simultaneous death and transfiguration. The little death in what Unamuno calls the 'genetic spasm' makes all things new again" (*The Immortalist*). Similarly, in Catholicism, we "die into life"; purification through the admission and *expression* of failure (sin). The revival meeting, the orgy, the rock concert are where people act out the profane to find the sacred. In protean performance, the "method" is not "internalization" but selective exhibition. Within this context, acting out is being the idea, not implying a relation to it. In America, the immense pressure to "conform," to "behave" (i.e., impersonate) leads to the kind of emotional and physical hiding that the protean performance—in its desire to *show* "where it is *at*" every moment—revolts against.

PLAYING THE GAME. . . . When internalization is high, there is often a feeling that the controls themselves are out of control—that emotion cannot be expressed when the individual would like to express it. Life is muted, experience filtered, emotion anesthetized, affective discharge incomplete. . . .— PHILIP SLATER, The Pursuit of Loneliness

---

The profane on stage and in life has its most serious roots in the protean impulse for transcendence. Grotowski has observed:

The theatre, when it was still part of religion, was already theatre: it liberated the spiritual energy of the congregation or tribe by incorporating myth and profaning or rather transcending it. The spectator thus had a renewed awareness of his personal truth in the truth of the myth and through fright and a sense of the sacred he came to catharsis. It was not by chance that the Middle Ages produced the idea of "sacral parody."

How we act out implies how we approach the world. Our moral attitudes and our view of what man is, are contained in how we present him. No matter with what style of acting we approach the stage or life, the mysterious duality of performance remains constant and significant. We are both in Time, and out of it; we are both part of history and continually reinventing it. This is how we grow, and how we remember. It is the reason for playing.

SETTINGS

Begin anew. Begin with your own building, the way the halls look, the way the light bounces. Think of the texture of the wall, of the smells natural to the building. Look out of the window.

Think of the hall, where you are hemmed in, or buoyed, or carried along, as the objects and the spaces change. Setting can astonish,

or lull,

or sing.

It can remove alternatives.

It can help to control.

When man begins to shape space, throwing a highway into the foreground, putting up a building, or erecting a stage flat, he does it in a certain "style," and that style evokes certain feelings.

What style is the building you're in? Is it, for instance, joyful and exuberant? Or is it more steel?

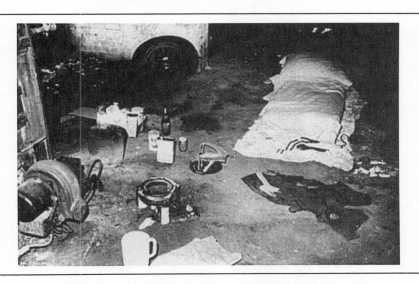

To become more aware of the ways the settings may affect you, ask certain simple questions. Does the setting change a great deal?
In what ways?

Is the setting built for human scale?

Even here we hear the maker behind. The playwright as a maker is different from other makers since he tends to work in as many dimensions as he can, and, with power, he will suggest new settings, new objects, or properties to hold in our hands, and create an entire miniature world, up on stage. Or if your office is the stage, the boss is a playwright in his own way, making up hoops through which his nearest allies jump, harassing the current pests, and posing before his own superiors. Or if your kitchen is the stage, you may be the playwright, making an environment out of wheat flour, sugar, or salt, with or without a stove.

The way we deal with our settings suggests our way of dealing with people, particularly when we begin to ask how actors are supposed to use the particular setting the playwright has invented. Do the actors use it a great deal, or does it tend to be a backdrop?

Even more important, in terms of functionality, do they possess it?

Or does it possess them?

Or worse, does it actually attack them?

In *The Silver Age,* a play by John Heywood, there is an environment which slashes with material, with scale, with change, and function, and space:

Hercules sinkes himselfe.
Flashes of fire;
the divels appeare at every corner
of the stage with several fire-workes.
The judges of hell, and the three sisters
run over the stage, Hercules
after them:
fire-workes all over the house.

By contrast, consider any skyscraper. It too is intended to awe. But the tone is different. Other sets, more public, seem more dignified, more powerful, more stern. Some are more dense. Others have a lot of levels and crevices.

Others are domes.
   Often there can be strong contrasts between areas, between materials, between levels, and between colors.

But sometimes the setting is all one continuous mass.

A section from *The Dream Play* by Strindberg shows the characters, standing in a hut.

LAWYER: *Like this door. When I close it, I open the way out, for you, Agnes.* (Goes out, closing the door)
DAUGHTER: *And now?*
(The scene changes. The bed with its hangings is transformed into a tent, the stove remaining. The new background shows a beautiful wooded shore, with beflagged

landing stages and white boats, some with sails set. Among the trees are little Italianesque villas, pavilions, kiosks, and marble statues)

In the middle distance is a strait.

The foreground presents a sharp contrast with the background. Burnt hillsides, black and white tree stumps as after a forest fire, red heather, red pigsties and outhouses. On the right is an open-air establishment for remedial exercises, where people are being treated on machines resembling instruments of torture.

On the left is part of the Quarantine Station; open sheds with furnaces, boilers, and pipes.

The DAUGHTER and the OFFICER are standing at the end of the previous scene.

The QUARANTINE MASTER, dressed now as a black-amoor, comes along the shore.

OFFICER (going up and shaking hands with the QUARANTINE MASTER) : *What? You here, old Gasbags?*

QUARANTINE MASTER : *Yes, I'm here.*

OFFICER : *Is this place Fairhaven?*

QUARANTINE MASTER : *No, that's over there.* (Points across the strait) *This is Foulstrand.*

OFFICER : *Then we've come wrong.*

The initial change, from a closed hut to an open space, seems summery with promise. Then it turns out we are limited to the foreground, a narrow strip of furnaces, boilers, pipes, and red blotched ground. The machines resemble torture racks. The new scene, exterior, full of detail, differs radically from what went before. But the kiosks seem almost unattainable. In the stage directions, Strindberg stresses the sharpness of the contrast and the painfulness. Those people are in a lurid nightmare, held back from all the trees, and homes that could give them rest.

The clarity, the sharpness, the vivid contrast of color, depth, and material, the disparity between the foreground where people walk in three dimensions, and the cardboard pavilions show us billboards of happiness. These are extremist contrasts. And the very wildness may express Strindberg's schizophrenic pain, at poverty, at the illnesses of his time, at men wanting—desperate, despite their talk, which remains determinedly flat. He blames greed and mothers. He is unfair : omits much of the forgiving jokes of daily life. This sparsity itself is a sign that we are dealing with a personal vision.

A vision, then : suggesting again that with walls as with faces, flat undifferentiated surfaces tell little. And in each play, whether the poet is crazy or sane, we are entitled to ask, how much human detail shows in the settings?

There it stands: thin as a razor, crazy in conventional terms, its slight leer, its angle of pride, not too good in design, but ours. (The thinness in fact suggests the level of significance.) Some detail, of course, is primarily symbolic.

Or is the whole setting, in its accumulation of detail, in some way symbolic?

Take an example from the Nazi occupation of France, Sartre's *The Flies*, a play created out of frustration at the cowardice of men faced with an invading tyrant. Zeus is berating Orestes. "The walls of the temple draw apart, revealing the firmament, spangled with wheeling stars. Zeus is standing in the background. His voice becomes huge—amplified by loud-speakers, but his form is shadowy."

ORESTES: *Let it crumble! Let the rocks revile me, and flowers wilt at my coming. Your whole universe is not enough to prove me wrong. You are the king of gods, king of stones and stars, king of the waves of the sea. But you are not the king of man.*
(The walls draw together. ZEUS comes into view, tired and dejected, and he now speaks in his normal voice)
ZEUS: *Impudent spawn! So I am not your king? Who, then, made you?*
ORESTES: *You. But you blundered; you should not have made me free.*
ZEUS: *I gave you freedom so that you might serve me.*
ORESTES: *Perhaps. But now it has turned against its giver. And neither you nor I can undo what has been done.*
ZEUS: *Ah, at last! So this is your excuse?*
ORESTES: *I am not excusing myself.*
ZEUS: *No? Let me tell you it sounds much like an excuse, this freedom whose slave you claim to be.*
ORESTES: *Neither slave nor master. I am my freedom.*

The original device, opening the walls of the temple to reveal a mighty vision behind, is straight out of the traditions of the Renaissance. "Cleave, solid rock, and bring the wonder forth!" Think of what it looks like, the vastness, the stars, the color, the panorama itself: surely this is detail on a cosmic scale, and full of marvels.

Sartre's device smacks of the Italian Renaissance, and, with the sound system, of modern political rallies, particularly those of Germany under Hitler. The language itself and the ideas are those of a neo-Platonic conception of God which evolved in the Renaissance, enforced, as Sartre sees it, with an almost Nazi terror. The suddenness of the change, the detail, the vastness, all this is intended to over-awe the individual.

It is clear Sartre feels that the individual can throw off all this. Orestes' attitude toward this "drama" is defiant. Sartre feels that we need only recognize the "theater" of such efforts to disengage. He points out also, how clearly we need to look at the various "dramatic settings" offered us, but he may be romantic. There may be no Zeus: but, on a human scale, are there not guns and howitzers, after the parade, to convince? Freeing ourselves of gods is easy, but of guns?

Sartre dreams of the power that one man, making his mind clear, could have. Existentialist and bitter as he is, Orestes is a dream of a playwright created for fellow prisoners in the German concentration camp—a fine conception—he would free the prisoners.

Focus is always an indication of attitude, like a spotlight. Who has the power; who should have our attention; and, what the maker respects. Watch how our focus point is shifted in this scene from *Indians*, by Arthur Kopit:

Act I: Scene 1.
BUFFALO BILL: *Be-before we start, I'd . . . just like to say—*
VOICE: *Bill!*
(The INDIANS slowly approach)
BUFFALO BILL: *—to say that . . . I am a fine man. And anyone who says otherwise is WRONG!*
VOICE (softly): *Bill, it's time.*

BUFFALO BILL: *My life is an open book; I'm not
ashamed of it's bein' looked at!*
VOICE (coaxing tone): *Bill . . .*
BUFFALO BILL: *I'm sorry, this is very . . . hard . . .
for me t' say. But I believe I . . . am a . . . hero . . . a
GODDAMN HERO!*
(Indian music).
    His horse rears wildly.
    Lights change for next scene.
       Light upon SITTING BULL. He is dressed simply—
no feathered headdress.
    It is winter.
SITTING BULL: *I am Sitting Bull! . . . In the moon of
the first snow-falling, in the year half my people died from
hunger, the Great Father sent three wise men . . . to
investigate the conditions of our reservation, though we'd
been promised he would come himself.*
(Lights up on SENATORS LOGAN, MORGAN, and
DAWES now: they are flanked by armed soldiers.
Opposite them, in a semi-circle, are SITTING BULL'S
people, all huddling in tattered blankets from the cold)
SENATOR LOGAN: *Indians! Please be assured that this
committee has not come to punish you or take away any of
your land but only to hear your grievances, determine
if they are just. And if so, remedy them. For we, like the
Great Father, wish only the best for our Indian children.*
(The SENATORS spread out various legal documents)

The play's creator is obviously focusing on remembering
the country, remembering what America has done, while
at the same time Buffalo Bill tries to gloss everything over,
and the Senators talk of the legality of their committee; the
impulse of Buffalo Bill is to make things simple, to turn it
all into a Wild West Show, with himself at the center, as a
hero. The author refuses, though, to let him stay in one
place. The lights change, the horse rears, the lights come
up on Sitting Bull—it is another focus—he is in a spare
robe, sometime in the past. Only after we have recognized
him and heard him for a moment does the author let the
lights come up further, on the committee—and a new view
of the problem. The play continues to shift its place, and
time. And the audience shares Buffalo Bill's reaction, which
is an attempt to deny, to defend, to stave off remembering
material that makes us seem human, or confused.

The play's shifts mimic consciousness and lead us rapidly
through the kind of blurs and recastings that are continually going on in our mind as we try to forget whatever
is painful. One way to resolve our doubts is to assert that
we are goddamn heroes. Goddamn: the word is deliberate:
the author has brought the focus in on Buffalo Bill, suffering, resembling ourselves.

The detail is simple: real robes, wood spears, a sketched-in set behind. We are not surrounded by "realistic" detail, into which we could fall, saying, yes, this is just the way it was. It isn't. It is a reproduction; it is Arthur Kopit, reflecting on what has gone by. The symbolic content of the individually highlighted details becomes heavier, then, as the evening goes on.

The change in settings, sudden, total, marked by a black pause between; the contrast between the Wild West Show opening, the contrast of neon and flashed metal, with the wood of the Indian town; the contrast in scale from the "theatrical" to the merely human are suggestive of Kopit's intentions. He is not unfriendly: but as a friend he will remind us of what we like to gloss over.

He is still up on a stage, "making a point." He is still arguing with us, using space, and body, and language, to convince us—hopefully with more humanity and depth than a "hero" does. But it is clearly still a play, to jolt us into some consciousness.

Buffalo Bill is in some ways a stand-in for the audience. He is surrounded by the Indians and his own past. Despite his attempts, the mind goes back, the setting changes, and the way it changes gives the mood to the play: one of the blood and the mind at work, on difficult truths.

Here is the end of *A Black Mass* by LeRoi Jones, which calls on its audience to join in prayers at the close:

JACOUB falls. The beasts howl and hop, and then, turning to the audience, their mouths drooling and making obscene gestures, they move out into the audience, kissing and licking people as they hop eerily out, still screaming: *White! . . . White! . . . Me . . . Me . . . Me . . . White!*
NARRATOR'S VOICE over loud-speaker with low drums and heavy trombones after beasts leave: *And so, Brothers and Sisters, these beasts are still loose in the world. Still they spit their hideous cries. There are beasts in our world, Brothers and Sisters. There are beasts in our world. Let us find them and slay them. Let us lock them in their caves. Let us declare the Holy War. The Jihad. Or we don't deserve to live. Izm-el-Azam. Izm-el-Azam. Ism-el-Azam. Ism-el-Azam.*
(Repeated until all lights black)   (Black)

The net effect of this is to cement the black members of the audience into an alliance, into an act of prayer, not determined to allow the beast to attack again; not to permit the whites to "move out into the audience, kissing and licking people as they hop eerily out, still screaming 'White! . . . White! . . . Me . . . Me . . . Me . . . White!' " With this setting we end up, deep and close, in the room which is totally black.

The setting takes us beyond words into the experiences which convince and propel men and women more than they generally would say. Space, prayer, the sounds, the light— all are shaped by one artist to express a rage he feels building inside each of the members of the audience. The style, and the intent, are obviously different from those of Kopit. Recognizing what is shared, Jones has gone beyond meditating with his audience, to jar, to pray, to help them join together in a new community. He has sanctified and emboldened the group: and they can hear this, and express this praying, and they can feel this, in blackness.

It is always worth imagining yourself a designer of new spaces. Think of trying to build the most horrible room you have even been in. What materials would you choose? At what scale? With how much light? Would people be able to stand on top of anything and use it—or would the room surround and overpower them? How much could people manipulate? Would it be deep? Complicated, in its levels, and spaces—or extremely simple? How would it change? Is there a lot of detail? Or is it all of one kind? Is there one focus? What, then, is celebrated in this room?

In most construction, planners and architects and engineers battle it out with politicians and unions and foremen; the building is always a compromise solution: but it does tend to express the net conclusion, the joint agreement, on what the building should be. It is, in a way, as clumsy as democracy: the sense of these people, these play-makers, gets through.

Never let anyone else tell you simply what a building is: it is your reaction that counts, and that is very complicated. The more you know about the setting, the more complex your reaction will be. Start by getting your gut-reaction.

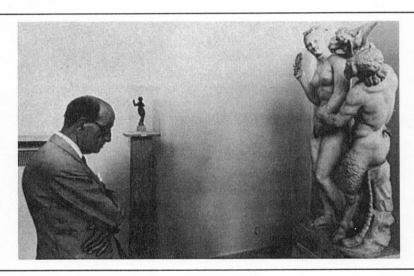

Once you know what your reaction is, you can begin to point to what has caused it—the walls, the view, the tone of the place. Then is the time to name the play-maker: and what he wants to do with his free play. Brutality will show itself, generally, as will humanity: and not in what the man is pretending to do, but in the unacknowledged cues he gives, as we all do, despite ourselves.

Setting is an expression: and a highway. Life shows. Open its map anywhere and begin again.

PROPERTIES

Properties are signs. Objects are all around us, but no one just happens to have *things* around:

There is a reason.

There is some "function"—but there is also an unacknowledged aspect: properties help to say part of who we are. A lot of attitudes get expressed: that old mug, the blue glasses, the memento from last summer's trip. Memories, feelings, a sense of your own past, a car, even, can do it.

Think of the properties in a play in an ordinary day. For properties can startle by sheer display.

Or properties can reflect profound contrasts.

At the same time properties can serve as a device for moving the plot forward.

Property is a language. There is a rhetoric. And the playwright is at the core, using the color, texture, material, focus, and scale in each object he slaps on stage.

Any familiar object has meanings, acquired over years of use in the culture. The playwright by his choice of objects and by his transformation of them reveals his personal attitudes. The way in which the playwright handles properties suggests the way he might want to be handling people.

If an object is stressed over a period of time, it comes to mean several different things.

Some playwrights attach meaning casually or callously. Such objects become expensive symbols.

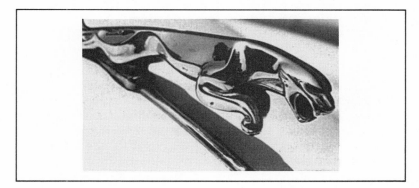

In the Renaissance, Queen Elizabeth was careful to make sure that all the signs of her office were scrupulously kept on view. Signs—symbols—give power.

In *The Jew of Malta*, the playwright, Christopher Marlowe, heaps a profusion of properties onto the stage.

BARABAS: *And thus methinks should men of*
  judgement frame
Their means of traffic from the vulgar trade,
And as their wealth increaseth, so enclose
Infinite riches in a little room.
But now how stands the wind?
Into what corner peers my halcyon's bill?
Ha! To the east? Yes; see how stands the vanes!
East and by south; why then I hope my ships
I sent for Egypt and the bordering isles
Are gotten up by Nilus' winding banks.
Mine argosy from Alexandria,
Loaden with spice and silks, now under sail,
Are smoothly gliding down by Candy shore
To Malta, through our Mediterranean sea.
But who comes here?   (Enter a MERCHANT)
                    How now?

The treasures of Barabas are a Mediterranean of riches. Barabas groups them by scale, then by shape. Different textures are hinted at, the colors listed. Barabas mentions place after place, adventure after adventure, form after form of money. Marlowe's way of handling the properties is blunt, sullen, rapacious: he grabs the thing, he shoves it forward, he talks about it—and then he forgets it.

Marlowe has a simple bold style for putting forward his properties: for attaching meaning to them: it is done in a stroke. Shakespeare contemplates things more.

In a few more minutes, the Governor of Malta will by legal feint try to take Barabas's goods, in "a legal theft," to pay off the Turks; other men groan under similar commands, and give in, muttering; but Barabas refused to give in, and in the course of the play he takes his revenge. In this way, Marlowe uses the treasures as a kind of *locus classicus*: this is where it all began.

In contrast, Harold Pinter uses props as tools.

An atmosphere of terror has been growing, and now we have a blackout. Dim lights through the window. DAVIES drops his matchbox and suddenly it is kicked.
DAVIES (muttering) : *Come on. Who's this? Who's this got my box?*
(Pause)
Who's in here?
(Pause)
I got a knife here. I'm ready. Come on then, who are you?
(He moves, stumbles, falls and cries out)
(Silence)
(A faint whimper from DAVIES. He gets up)
All right!
(He stands. Heavy breathing)
(Suddenly the Electrolux starts to hum. A figure moves with it, guiding it. The nozzle moves along the floor after DAVIES, who skips, dives away from it, and falls, breathlessly) *Ah, ah, ah, ah, ah, ah! Get away-y-y-y!* (The Electrolux stops)

Quite a distance from Barabas's treasure—to this vacuum cleaner. The noise seems malevolent, though, and seems to come from some vague, unidentifiable engine of torture. By taking the machine out of its ordinary setting, Pinter has endowed his machine with some rather frightening characteristics. By putting it in the darkened room, when a man enters thinking himself alone and then cannot turn on the lights, which is bothersome enough, by making the machine begin after several moments of gawked terror, and then by having it move toward him growling, with one part clanking against the floor, Pinter engineers a terrible mechanical joke on his character. Then—in a flash—the lights go on.

We see that it is just a vacuum cleaner. But is it? What of the hate on the part of Mick, the man who has been anonymously terrorizing Davies? Mick is sinister, despite the fact that he says a moment later that he didn't mean any harm—that he was just doing a bit of spring cleaning. At night. In the dark. Against Davies.

The vacuum cleaner is symbolic, but in a utilitarian style. The vacuum cleaner does not appear again in the play (it is tucked under the bed after this) and it is not mentioned directly after this scene. In comparison to Barabas's riches, then, it would seem at first a very minor element in the play. It is not a traditional emblem, nor is it a simple symbol, it is a tool: it furthers the plot. What else are tools for?

Pinter talks of the moment of astonishment when suddenly "ordinary" reality takes on some threatening new tone. Until we figure out what that is, and adjust ourselves to it, we feel terror. And Pinter aims for such moments. He is doing to us what he does to Davies—with a prop.

Meanings can be attached to properties in many different ways. Most people, for instance, are quite perfunctory at times, almost "labeling" the property with the several qualities they want us to notice in it—my shiny new coat, my damn old boots—just pasting a label on it. Other playwrights, wiser, involve the property in minor action. Or

with a certain *élan*, they wrench it out of its normal context by violence. Or, still more oblique, the playwright may have the object referred to by a series of different characters unobtrusively throughout the play, as the sea gull is in Chekhov's work. We need to know then, as a measure of the man's depth, what means of symbolizing the playwright uses.

Is he assertive—or violent? Or does he have confidence enough in what he is saying to let the meaning grow? Or does it have to be said fast and hard, and damn all other considerations? There is always a problem, too, of simplicity.

Has he just borrowed a traditional emblem, like a crown, or a throne? Does he just grab it and expect you to really bow down to it, as if he himself had expressed all the "meanings" that crown, or that key, holds in our culture? He is short-handing.

Or, more flowery, a man may use a property merely because it is bright, and pleases him, and has no further point than that. In an entertainment, in any extravagance, some pleasure is gratuitous.

But we are dealing once again with his intentions, with what kind of a play he is trying to write, what level of seriousness he is operating on; and, if he is serious, it will appear in the particular way he handles properties. Look quickly at the evidence.

See how a man's tone comes out, as he regards a scene on a heath, or a claustrophobic house in Norway trapping a woman. The amount of meaning a playwright finds—and endows—in a property suggests how much meaning he is trying to communicate, and of what kind.

The test of the person who uses properties, then, is not really in "what they mean," though that is of some importance; it is in the way the person uses them, in what this suggests about the person's thoughtfulness in general. In each play there is a different style of properties, much as there is a distinct style of language. Watch an object become a religious springboard, during García Lorca's mourning at the end of *Blood Wedding*. Four men bring in the coffin, and deposit the two bodies in front of the cross. Two men are dead, over one bride, who weeps in the back, in front the mother calls to the neighbors.

BRIDE: *And this is a knife,*
a tiny knife
that barely fits the hand;
fish without scales, without river,
so that on their appointed day, between two
*   and three,*
with this knife,
two men are left stiff,
with their lips turning yellow.

MOTHER: *And it barely fits the hand*
but it slides in clean
through the astonished flesh
and stops there, at the place
where trembles enmeshed
the dark root of a scream.
(THE NEIGHBORS, kneeling on the floor, sob)
CURTAIN.

It turns out you cannot entirely control small objects. You can discern that which is important, and raise that to the notice of others. You can remind them, violently, or quietly, or with overwhelming detail, of the things that single property reminds you of, sufferings you feel are important to them, to all of us.

Add up the signs. Sometimes they are as obvious as a sea gull being purity or faith forever and ever, sometimes they are original—it was in an arbor in the *Spanish Tragedy* that Hieronimo died again. Sometimes we care about how the playwright deals with properties, and always we care about how the playwright deals with us. Properties are an inheritance, objects showing how people have been at work on their environment: the real estate.

COSTUME

ostume too is a set of signs: a language, a miniature world to play within.

Imagine that you had a world almost free of culture. No schools; no taboos; no expected form of dress.

Imagine the shapes of costumes that would be possible, ballooning, shining,

mushrooming,

barreling forward.

You could wear wings, or swords, amulets, and a sixteen-foot train of silk; you could wear nothing, except a white pearl.

Color as well: mahogany reds, turquoise, amethysts of green, a swath of vermilion. Yellow, in all its forms: not just the ones in cloth today, but those of the skin, the natural pollen, the sands.

You could decide that your entire wardrobe ran in gray

one day, then purple, or ocher for another day: that one day everyone you met would be like you, or in a variation on that hue; or within your own costume, no matter what

size it may have grown to by now, variety, or blandness, a riffle of contrasts, or a single bold orange.

Perhaps grass would suit, as material, or glass, or brick-red ceramic, held in place by chains. The texture of your costume matters; it gives a sign of how much you like to feel, whether you wear too smooth lingerie, or scratchy hair shirts on your day off, whether you aim to be indifferent to the sensation, or indulge yourself, moderately, in velvet. Think what other textures you might like: a vinyl layer holding you like skin? A shirt feeling like water? Or like warm sand, moving down over you? Or a jacket dangling with accouterments that only you can define for sure?

Costumes protect and yet reveal.

Plays curve us free of the culture of the straightened line, freedom wherein is rich gold.

Wear what you want, then. But why does our culture care? Because costume expresses so much. In one small way our own costumes, invented at random, bought almost by chance, show in very fine ways that we agree or disagree with others.

A powerful playwright, of course, has even more freedom—he can invent whole uniforms. Or he can distinguish each character.

He can create baroque variety: or, like IBM, he can make a distinct style of costuming prevalent for a large corps. Someone who only thought about costume might dress everyone at work like this:

Clothing may or may not reflect the body or the person inside of it: it depends on their freedom.

Costume can lie, magnificently: it can assert that the character is strong and loves her body when she actually is afraid and ashamed of it. But wearing the right clothes can sometimes lead a character on to realize that she is aware, and is proud. Then she can even relish her own body, in its motions, under or outside of linen. Body tights, jeans, bikinis, open dresses, each says something about what she likes doing, about the way she likes to do it, whether slowly, or gradually, with surprise, coming into full energy after a more gradual beginning, or just with a constant grace. A character has her own style in clothing, and, even more important, her own style of showing it, or not showing any, before the world. Stand naked and think what it would feel like to have all your clothes on, all the ones you own, at once.

Here is a scene from Brecht's *Galileo*, which involves a man getting dressed in robes. In the end he stands partially revealed as the Pope.

A chamber in the Vatican. THE POPE, URBAN VIII: A pause.

POPE: *These shuffling feet are making me nervous.*

INQUISITOR: *May they be more telling than my words, Your Holiness. Shall all these go from you with doubt in their hearts?*

POPE: *This man has friends. What about Versailles? What about the Viennese court? They will call Holy Church a cesspool for defunct ideas. Keep your hands off him.*

INQUISITOR: *In practice it will never get far. He is a man of the flesh. He would soften at once.*

POPE: *He has more enjoyment in him than any man I ever saw. He loves eating and drinking and thinking. To excess. He indulges in thinking-bouts! He cannot say no to an old wine or a new thought.* (Furious) *I do not want a condemnation of physical facts. I do not want to hear battle cries: Church, church, church! Reason, reason, reason!* (Pause)

*These shuffling feet are intolerable. Has the whole world
come to my door?*
INQUISITOR: *Not the whole world, Your Holiness. A select
gathering of the faithful.*
(Pause)
POPE (exhausted): *It is clearly understood: he is not to
be tortured.*
(Pause)
At the very most, he may be shown the instruments.
INQUISITOR: *That will be adequate, Your Holiness. Mr.
Galilei understands machinery.*
(The eyes of Barberini look helplessly at the CARDINAL
INQUISITOR from under the completely assembled panoply
of POPE URBAN VIII).

Contrast: simple and strong, between the loose easy
movements of the man before elevation, and the trapped
eyes afterward. Ceremony and sparseness: Brecht uses the
blunt broad style of costuming, etching the scene out clearly
so his words will be able to move in their usual complexity
of style and thought to the indictments he wishes to make.

The two styles—of handling costume, of handling language—come together in one moment. Brecht uses each
element differently—with one driving into the other at his
climax. He does so partly to point a moral, and partly to
show how one man is caught—by his ideas, his culture, and
their accumulated garb—in a situation only his mind could
free him from.

Costumes reveal powers, in a person, and their own
response to those abilities, those beauties, the powers of
nature. During the scene our eyes are directed toward one
thing throughout: the enrobement. Physically, a large
change takes place at a stately pace, taking Barberini from
thin homespun to brocade upon silk upon velvet—symbols
are hung around him like beads. The extra robes represent
accusations Brecht has in mind. That costume is huge.
It is a display worth looking at. Clearly Brecht has more
in mind than a simple miracle.

In a play written in the 1550's Ralph Roister Doister,
who has bragged a lot about what a soldier he is, now
faces the house of a woman he thinks has insulted him, by
not accepting his bid for her love. He comes in with two
drummers, and flags, and some friends.

ROISTER DOISTER: *I lack yet an headpiece.*
MERRYGREEK: *The kitchen pail—the best hence to
Greece,
Run, fetch it, Dobinet, and come at once withal,
And bring with thee my potgun, hanging by the wall!*
(Exit DOUGHTY)
I have seen your head with it full many a time

Covered as safe as it had been with a screen;
And I warrant it save your head from any stroke,
Except perchance to be amazed with the smoke;
I warrant your head therwith—except for the mist—
As safe as if it were fast locked up in a chest,
And lo, here our Dobinet cometh with it now!

(DOUGHTY brings the pail)
DOUGHTY: *It will cover me to the shoulders well enow.*
MERRYGREEK: *Let me see it on.*
ROISTER DOISTER: *In faith, it doth meetly well.*
MERRYGREEK: *There can be no fitter thing. Now ye
must us tell What to do.*
ROISTER DOISTER: *Now forth in array, sirs! and
stop no more!*
MERRYGREEK: *Now Saint George to borrow! Drum,
dub-a-dub afore!—NICHOLAS UDALL*

Here a man is talking in a bold, ranting style, while actually putting on a kitchen bucket as a helmet. The clothes undermine the pose, and guarantee that we see him the way he really is. Despite the bloated heroism the language shows he is an ass.

The clothes encourage an attack on bad literary style— the pail marks romantic talk as so much slop.

It is rapid, and grotesque. Its humor is from the tavern, from drunks. The language is ornate as any medieval romance. In a certain lightness, the scene and the costume have performed the perfect *reductio ad absurdum* of the rhetoric—and they have guaranteed that we sense the essential lightness of the play, despite all the heaviness of the language.

Language plays off against costume, in every play, as it does against each other element, like settings, or properties; a character may start talking quietly, but the clothes show he is loud. We are a complex of styles.

Molière, a man whose every play shows him delighting in his costumes, with an almost Mozartian joy in them, has a certain loose, and casual way of choosing a "style" of costume for a given character. Working in the after-thought of the Renaissance, perusing, and adapting, he can evoke small changes in a lace that undermine a peasant's attempt to pass for an aristocrat, or even a bourgeois. At times he flings a costume before us for the fun of it. Then he points out another sad division standing between the way a man talks, a style which can be learned, and the way he dresses, which because the distinctions are so fine and so little noticed can offer a great deal more difficulty to the amateur. Monsieur Jourdain, for instance, is a man who cares very heartily about this matter.

The merchant who has hired a dancing master and a music master to teach him how to move in "high society" keeps blundering through his lessons, according to them: but they like his money, and so kowtow to him, no matter what he says or does. When he enters, he is dressed in a ludicrously lush striped dressing gown, lined with green and orange, and he is accompanied by two lackeys, signs of his new-found "elegance."

M. JOURDAIN: *Lackeys. Hey, my two lackeys!*
FIRST LACKY: *What do you wish, sir?*
M. JOURDAIN: *Nothing. I just wanted to see if you hear me all right.* (To the two MASTERS) *What do you think of my servants' liveries?*
DANCING MASTER: *Magnificent.*
M. JOURDAIN (opens his dressing gown, displaying tight red-velvet breeches, and a short green-velvet jacket):

*And here's a little sports costume to do my exercises in,
in the morning.*
MUSIC MASTER: *Very smart.*
M. JOURDAIN: *Lackey!*
SECOND LACKEY: *Yes, sir?*
M. JOURDAIN: *Here, hold my gown.* (He removes his
gown) *How do you like me this way?*
DANCING MASTER: *Splendid. It couldn't be more perfect.*
M. JOURDAIN: *Now let's have your little business.*
MUSIC MASTER: *First, I should like to have you hear
a composition which this young man here has just done
for the serenade you ordered. He is one of my pupils; he is
very gifted for this sort of thing.*
M. JOURDAIN: *Yes; but you shouldn't have had it done
by a pupil. You aren't too good to do the job yourself.*
MUSIC MASTER: *Don't let the word "pupil" put you off,
sir. Such pupils as this know as much as the greatest
masters; and the melody is as lovely as it can be. Just
listen.*
M. JOURDAIN: *Give me my dressing gown so I can
listen better. . . . Wait a minute, I think it will be better
without the dressing gown. . . . No, give it back to me. It'll
be better that way.—The Bourgeois Gentleman*

And finally, after more fussing with his dressing gown,
the song begins. We know that Monsieur Jourdain is trying to pretend he is a gentleman. We do not know much
more about him before he enters; hence it is primarily this
context with which we view his entrance. And what do we
see? An extravagance of ribbons and silk. There is the
obvious fact of luxury here, and bright colors, the fact that
Monsieur Jourdain has *two* layers of clothing on, the fact
that he has two different types of clothing on, one loose,
one tight—and both rich: in addition to operating as a
sign of Monsieur Jourdain's attempts at "nobility," the
clothing is visually delightful in itself as sheer show.

Monsieur Jourdain's aims, his hopes, are expressed in
his sports costume. But Molière will not dwell on this long.
He uses the costuming—in its flare, and in its excess—to
brighten the scene.

And in other plays another playwright might show us
a series of people in ripped mill sacks, and patches of
animal skin, the raw style showing us our real condition,
calmly. Or furiously. Or one might merely show a national
hero yellow and red and shining in an epic of swords, arrows,
and guns, while talking diffidently about the need to imagine
such things. Thinking of Brecht, thinking of Udall, thinking of Molière: each chooses a certain style of clothing, for
his own reasons: in his own tone—whether of outrage, or
blunt satire, or humor; or in other plays, regret, or an urge

to overawe us, by mere excellence of cloth. How he presents things—not just the particular style—makes a difference, the ear still listening for a human voice.

Even from clothes, then, and the way men wear them, we can get a sense of the way they approach us, the as-yet-unknown audience. For a playwright chooses the style of costume in order to say something about his character; then also because he enjoys the style for some reason and wants to show it to us: and it is at this point the manner of presenting becomes important.

With what outrage Udall shows us that helmet! With what amusement Molière his double dressing gown, and tights! Strindberg is more dour.

The NURSE takes the CAPTAIN to a chair. He slumps down. She picks up the strait-jacket, and goes behind the chair. BERTHA, his child, creeps out.

NURSE: *Mr. Adolf, do you remember when you were my dear little boy, and I used to tuck you up at night and say your prayers with you? And do you remember how I used to get up in the night to get you a drink when you were thirsty? And how, when you had had dreams and couldn't go to sleep again, I'd light the candle and tell you pretty stories. Do you remember?*

CAPTAIN: *Go on talking, Margaret. It soothes my mind. Go on talking.*

NURSE: *Aye, that I will, but you listen carefully. D'you remember how once you took a great big kitchen knife to carve a boat with, and I came in and had to trick the knife away from you? You were such a silly little lad, one had to trick you, you never would believe what anyone did was for your own good.... "Give me that snake," I said, "or else he'll bite you." And then, see, you let go of the knife.* (Takes the revolver from his hand) *And then, too, when it was time for you to dress yourself, and you wouldn't. I had to coax you, and say you should have a golden coat and be dressed just like a prince. Then I took*

*your little tunic, that was just made of green wool, and
held it up in front of you and said: "In with your arms,
now, both together."* (Gets the strait-jacket on) *And then
I said: "Sit nice and still now, while I button it up
behind."* (Ties the sleeves behind him) *And then I said:
"Up with you, and walk across the floor like a good boy,
so Nurse can see how it fits."* (Leads him to the sofa)
And then I said: "Now you must go to bed."
CAPTAIN: *What's that? Go to bed, when I'd just been
dressed? My God! What have you done to me?* (Tries to get
free) *Oh you fiendish woman, what devilish cunning!
Who would have thought you had the brains for it?* (Lies
down on the sofa)—*The Father*

The Captain cries out when he wakes up too late. Strindberg himself feels trapped by the costume: and he uses it,
simplistically, physically, like a net to capture the audience,
to guarantee that his audience will sympathize with the
poor Captain. We, in the audience, may resent his being
so simplistic, so dim about the minds of people, but Strindberg's rage is of a kind with the Captain's here: it is the
outrage of a small child, howling—and it will not stop until
he chooses such a simple, bold, violent image. It expresses
that much anger. And he chooses that image, that style,
because he wants in some way to shake us.

Stepping out of clothes has traditionally been an invitation to love. Even our decoration reveals our choices. Deprived of clothes, we would be deprived, in a way, of the
cloth of expression.

GESTURE

The body is where we begin each day.

One sharp gesture may express our most undifferentiated feelings, about ourselves, about our life, about the way in which, ultimately, we see ourselves reaching out to others, and responding to their unceasing touch.

How we accept pleasure, how we reject fear, how we overcome a hundred intricacies of a daily intercourse with others: all these may be sketched by our body as it turns.

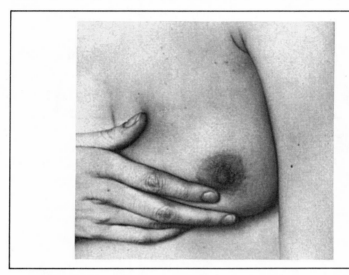

Like soul written in flesh, the play in gesture leads us on to ecstasies. For gesture involves us in our real selves and in real love, and what her body is doing is therefore also in an important way our first clue to what she is really feeling, despite her talk, her rhetoric.

And we can pick up an incredible range of insight in a few seconds. Think, we take in what the gesture itself is, noticing how quickly it is done, how rhythmically, how

much actual strength is put into it, the sheer degree of physicality, and the movement and variation all under their clothes, in their particular environment.

For the body is obedient to each of our impulses. Of course, with just physical activity, we cannot achieve all that our bodies, and our beings want. We must take thought, and we must talk, and act, with others. This requires lines of action, and characters that we can assume or drop at our convenience. If one is in conflict with another, you have the argument or debate which is living personality.

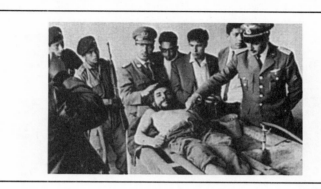

Again, everything comes together in the physical. All the modes—sets, properties, costumes, gestures—all are languages, and each at times expresses part of us in turn. But physical movement, this is our primary language. Not our truest, necessarily, or our deepest, but certainly our most brilliant and physically satisfying, and the one that most immediately says what the ideas and words must later act to explicate. Ideas, ultimately, are more important than the body, but character shows, at first notice, in the stance.

And the playwright, talking, to express his feelings through his characters, shows them with the gestures revealing inner character.

The playwright chooses this particular style of gesture to align some of his characters—say it is rigid, and military, with cigars—say it is cool and blue and disciplined with no hint of the cigar—to express his attitudes about us and to make us do things, certainly, to think certain things, but more, to confirm his own very personal view of the world.

Shakespeare, of course, loves bodies in all sorts of motion, and even in their fight against death, a battle which for him, at times, goes on after the body has stopped, but that is Shakespeare.

In any play these motions can seem dangerous to us: for we have a tendency when we see others doing something to get that same feeling in ourselves. Watching Punch and Judy punch and smash each other, breaking brickbats over each other's skulls, jamming legs, fingers, loose flesh under knives, glass, angle irons, and the front door, our body begins to think of all that feeling in ourselves.

Or watching some activity we like, whether dancing or artillery practice or simply people touching, our body begins to feel exhilarated, almost as if we had done that one leap without effort, or taken hands, with one strong gesture, without even having stirred from our seats.

Think for a moment of a Sergeant in the Marines. When someone is accustomed to staying where he is, without moving much, he needs some way of getting over the inexpressible feelings that come up. And he may stage shows with live human beings as actors to unleash those impulses, when he feels unable any other way to squash or redirect them. Here, for instance, is a scene from *The Brig*:

GRACE: *Private first class Lintz, I think the maggots are out of shape. Put them through an exercise drill.*
LINTZ comes in from the other side of the Brig. He enters the compound and stands inside the door with his arms folded.
LINTZ: *I want all the racks moved to the far end of the compound on the double. Then I want you in two ranks, a body length apart facing me.* (The prisoners pick up all the double cots and move them into a corner one against the other, leaving a considerable space in the middle of the inside compound. They then occupy the space in two ranks, a body length from one another) *All right, my bald children, down in the push-up position. By my count, one, two, one, two, one, two . . .* (He continues until the prisoners are all struggling and contorting to make the semblance of the exercise) *On your feet. Sit-up position. By my count, one, two, one, two, one, two . . .* (Again, he continues until they are exhausted) *On your feet. Start running in place, and you better get those legs up.* (The prisoners are running in place, kicking their legs high in the air) *On your bellies. On your feet. On your backs. You better get down when I tell you, maggots.—KEN BROWN*

The officer in charge is stern. The prisoners yell when they are told to, bowing, repeating, re-experiencing, like engines being revved, exercise after exercise, counted, timed, blocked into rhythm. Then, abruptly, arbitrarily, the rhythm is changed, the action shifts, the natural flow is lost: shot to pieces, if possible, by this playwright's own ironic imitation of military. It is known rule, as discipline, if you are at all sympathetic, or, if you are aching from just thinking about it, rough power, crushing any individual movement before it has a chance. Here is a condensation, the style of armies, from the days of Alexander the Great, callous, absurd, necessary, but punishing.

Moving in a style which is as sexual, as savage, and as brutal as its own, the Living Theater must therefore hint at its attitude toward the material—and, in a double-edged way, its attitude toward us.

In gesture, then, we often see the tenor of the character and if we consider it carefully, the tenor of the playwright as well, who chooses such a peculiar style for his characters, or for some of them. Each playwright draws us in by our own body's empathy. Then if he is wise the playwright turns us so we can see where these particular impulses may have taken us, or what they mean.

Macbeth, confronted at the end of the battle with Macduff, refuses to give up, despite the fact that all the prophecies are coming true, despite the fact that Macduff is the man the witches predicted would kill him:

MACBETH: *I will not yield*
To kiss the ground before young Malcolm's feet,
And to be baited with the rabble's curse.
Though Birnam wood be come to Dunsinane,
And thou opposed, being of no woman born,
Yet I will try the last: before my body
I throw my warlike shield: lay on, Macduff;
And damn'd be him that first cries 'Hold, enough!'
Exeunt, fighting. Alarums

Macbeth goes down fighting, and his last gesture with the shield up, sword in hand, sticks in our memories; here is a man refusing to surrender. Slow to get involved in the initial plot, Macbeth now drives past any retreat. The situation tightens around him. This is the moment in which his whole life is put to the test. He emerges with his sword drawn, knowing he will die.

If he had relented, we would have turned against him in contempt, being as unforgiving as most audiences; we might have thought his career a barreling melodrama, murder, the throne, more murder, and in the end cowardice and defeat. Macbeth learns to ignore his lesser soul: like charity, caution has passed out of him. Macbeth complains, a few lines earlier, of prophecies that puzzle us "in a double sense." In his end Macbeth has given up that uncertainty.

These actions are simple and not repeated: they are also of a certain speed and will, and because of that determination, they may take on a certain scale. Small, rapid clutchings at his dagger would make the man seem weak; even now, pressed to the edge, Macbeth will not go nervous. The body is still unbendable—and it is the whole body that is involved in these two gestures, bringing the shield up front, as he prepares, regripping the sword. His feet take the stance, and leap into action; right after the speech, the conflict will use up his whole strength. A life, then, and a unique style of action.

That action charging into Macduff, even when he knows Macduff will kill him in a minute's time, affirms Macbeth's self, whatever that is. We do not know what it is. We remember, though, the action itself—and feel it—and then begin, after the play, to look back within it for some clue to what went wrong, to some indication of the way in which a man as kind as this became a murderer and would not stop. Gesture contains so much it grows ambiguous.

Look now at a scene from a mystery play written in the late Middle Ages, by the anonymous Wakefield Master. It shows Christ being put on the cross.

FIRST TORTURER (As they string Christ up on the cross):

Yet draw out this arm and make it fast,
With this rope, that well will last,
And each man lay hand to.
SECOND TORTURER: *Next drive a nail there through,*
And then we shall nothing doubt,
For it will not burst.
THIRD TORTURER: *That shall I do, so might I stand!*
FIRST TORTURER: *Hold down his knees.*
SECOND TORTURER: *That shall I—*
His nurse did never better do.
Lay on with each hand.
FIRST TORTURER: *Hold it now fast there*
One of you the bore shall bear,
And then it may not fail.
SECOND TORTURER: *Yea, and bring it to the mark.*
THIRD TORTURER: *Pull pull!*
(They begin to raise the cross, straining and grunting)
FIRST TORTURER: *Have now!*
SECOND TORTURER: *Let see!*
THIRD TORTURER: *Aha!*

The language is as innocent and as rhythmic as a child's chant—and as indifferent, given the actual actions described, and the way they are performed, one after another, almost like a job, but with a certain relish. It is not realistic either, being so organized by the rhetoric. It is only a representation: it is an emblem of the real. But what realities—of the torturers' real bodies, their sweat, the way they handled the arms, the leg, nailing, cursing, lifting. Ponder the raw physicality hinted at, in contrast to the blandness of what we see: and throughout it all, the consciousness that this, for audience and actor, was God's only Son.

A gesture is like a bas-relief: on a coin, say, the figure of the Duke in a small medieval town, proud only as the most powerful can be. He looks out at you. Years of his active stands toward life bulge from his jaw: you can almost sense how he habitually stood. "In deed, as in the face," an old Italian proverb, meaning, that what we do, the way we habitually move our head, will register, in the bones, until the face takes on the new shape.

You can see it on the subway: men whose lives have settled into a set of permanent begrudging, or permanent lament, or a sort of sullen slump—gestures toward death.

Or toward Dionysius.

Images of the twirls of your own imagination, the dreams you once had; the exact way you turned, once, when you were eight; then again, at your first dance, or in sports, or certain beds, underneath loving. For we love, loving, and the gestures, or the words, are only signs trying to describe what went on.

Signs are how we exist. This much is obvious.

IDEAS
ARE
SIGNS

The turn of his walk, the balance of her soft leg, for a moment, in sun. The heads tossed at angles, singing, and then laughing. Each day a sign changes slightly in what it can say; each slogan, repeated, changes; each jacket, worn a day, changes. The thing itself remains the same. What changes is what the thing is a sign of.

Using words is a major way of fighting a change in a sign. So the body slips away at times to say what *it* has to say.

As Whitman said, the self is multiple. Alas, we are always expressing it all every moment. This much is obvious. We should, if we had sense, realize that if we are by our subterfuges, even, our costumes, even, showing exactly what we try now to hide, then we should start realizing that we do not ever succeed in hiding anything—so it might as well show.

Playwrights use artificial gestures to tell us about societies, about traits below the surface of our more ordinary masks. We could all be dancing, if we would, or we could be destroying each other's bodies, like hyenas, if we were not masked. Repression is only a redirection of energy. Most people break out of those feelings, and most people act with an ease and an agility none of these figures could accurately match, if they were uniform.

The self *is* multiple. We are expressing all every moment.

This stance, that stance, your walk sums up what you are feeling right now. It is your own; your own attitude toward yourself, toward what is possible for you, in mind and body is expressed in the way you move.

Think of a Dionysian gesture. All is a sign, the oracles once said.

Gestures are signs that serve to suck us into a given plot that we enjoy: and herein lies their danger. Gestures are signs that hint at plots and characters we would enjoy associating ourselves with, even if it cost us money, or our ease, or our cynicism, or our days.

In the beginning was the sign, and the sign was with God, begins one story about Christ. Dionysians drink deep.

PLOT

Plots give hope to the world.

A playwright is someone who has put on stage a spectacle of himself in contact with the world. Some artists feel like Atlas. And they are as honest as any man, trying as best they can, to tell what is wrong, or best, what can be done, if anything, and if nothing, how we may be. Think, for a moment, of another action.

A plot is a way of understanding what is going on, and we all have used it that way—tossing out malign conspiracies, dangling charges, outridden by men we did not think of, succeeding, ultimately, by being ourselves.

I stress the self in the actual construction, speaking to you, because it is where the stories begin. In bone and beauteous brain, in one word, in what the playwright says, in how he loves you, or thinks of you, or what he dislikes, what pleases him. In what he does, in all these impulses, there are some very strong wants. We ignore them at our peril. Blocked, by fear, by "logic" or havoc, these feelings move toward other regions—emerging as productions of the spirit, enjoyable as such.

Good plots tell a great deal. At first the hero meets three witches, hears a prophecy, believes it, and therefore seizes the crown, then has to war with his own impulses, fighting always against the right, against his own knowledge that he should never have begun: but he will not have another word about that, he will go back into battle, again and again, and then he will be killed, and by the end of the play that tall, rotten-red Scotchman, Macbeth is dead, and we are thinking "Why couldn't he have gone on and won?" or "What has he been through?" or, really, "What have we been through together in being drawn into such a plot?" The self remembers things in plots, as you can see, made metallic, in emblems:

A bridge, a way in and out, we interpret it quickly for its use: where it takes us, how it is built, how it would shake under us. Plot, then, is a way of planning. Think, for instance, of what a certain friend is going to do for the next few minutes, and project a plot. Dull, perhaps, just a person sitting, and reading, a short plot—not anything to be too worried about. But then, think of his next few weeks, think about those plans he might deny about the more distant future. We are imagining our friend forward, through a series of decisions and actions, handling a number of emotional problems, which may or may not be solvable, facing risk each moment, and solving it by plotting or imagining. The incidents that make us feel the way we do: that is what goes into a plot, at its base.

A plot is a way of testing the self in the imaginary world. Julius Caesar, planning, before coming back to Rome. Churchill each day during blitz. Mao or Che before their entry into battle, planning, developing themselves by foreseeing obstacles and encountering them, thereby training themselves in what must be overcome—almost as a discipline or a manual of battles. Imagine what you will: a way of avoiding terrible rats, or a way of paddling home to paradise. Plots seem free but they lead us into life.

Each plot is a possibility, refined each day in contact
with the world, but essentially perpetual; each shows a
sense of the real self, in contact with the world, in this
active mood, say, or that unfolding mist of regrets and
memories, elaborating a full scenario in half a moment—
then pain intrudes and makes the plot more realistic.

In watching a tragic scene the audience is eager to
believe. It dislikes a tragedy that cannot bear up under
common sense. And when an audience first watches comic
scenes, too, it may enjoy the nature of the attack, and
therefore want to maintain belief in that, too. Our eager-
ness to believe a plot is a measure of our desperate need
for expression, whether in political or literary theater, our
need to change our lives; and, even more, our personal
silence. And someone else's plot may be built so well we
voluntarily step into it, for a while, to satisfy those feelings.

By relying on other people's plots we enter the dilemmas

of the world. A good dictator always makes a good show and sucks some people in to join in a crusade or a task he has proclaimed, and this maintains him in power. Other people resent his brutality or his indifference and rise up, calling others to join in a higher task.

The world is a maze of plots, and to know each man we must know all of these plots. And think how complex man is, how his impulses run counter to one another, how chaotic he is. It is little wonder that he runs amok among the possibilities he opens up to himself, or gets locked into one same story over and over, for its possibilities, or risks all in one crusade, to kill or be killed, and succeeds. So many stories, so many lives.

Our ordinary lives seem unremarkable: it is the shape of each life that is unique.

Dostoevski went to prison and was lined up to be killed. He was not shot though, and he lived out the rest of his life explaining, atoning, and drinking to celebrate that he did not get killed, that he was still alive and in Russia. That is one story of his life. Another is, of course, the journalist. Another is the man who made a number of large gambles, and won big and lost big. These are all plots of his, stripped, though, of his unique voice. And it is in his own voice that he tells us what he sees, in making up novels, in plots he felt summed up his own experiencing of the world. Some men use cannon, instead.

Heading an army back from exile into his own country with the aid of allies he despised, taking control, letting it go, condemning France for her weakness. Retiring, then returning to power to stop civil war. He stops the war, kills a number of men, and pulls the country's army out of its former colonies: an achievement, something he worked out, risking everything over and over again. But what was de Gaulle? One cannot say. He was only a man, we say, challenging, and reshaping, and building. The country, the cemeteries, the society of Algeria tell of some of his plots, even now.

Or Marx. An idea, a set of techniques, a series of actions which Marx anticipated: the Russian Revolution, the Chinese, the transformation of people's thinking, for over a hundred years—not quite as he originally expected. The world tells all of his best plots in its own way, over and over.

The intention of a plot is to sum up a man's life, to examine how he encountered the world, to express his feelings, to see how one line of action might succeed or fail. We find one act, or one set of acts, reveals all—if it is properly explicated by the rest of the play. The plot is the core of our attention. Will Romeo and Juliet's love go well? Will Ophelia and Desdemona and Cleopatra and their lovers survive in love?

How strong is the plot? How thick or thin? Does it
consider situations and issues which are important, or does
it merely pick up certain issues in order to fling us along in
the excitement of the combat? What themes does the playwright raise? Abstract nouns are just codes for what comes
underneath: justice, freedom, liberation, discipline, order,
ecstasy's sweet possibility. Plots wear out, in the tradition
of the theater, as each new interpreter devours one, and

puts it back out, a skeleton only moved by new flesh.

Che's diary imagines and projects the maps, the cross-
ings, days off in La Paz. The ruinous mountains. The truck
by the stream; days of no noise except the wind, and men
bitching, and hard work. Then an ambuscade. The facts
are as grass: it is the patterning we each remake of the
facts—as enemies or as comrades—that determines their
significance. The shaping grows out of our own experience
of the street we live on, and the wash of our newscasts.
Each time we think of an extraordinary person we imagine
a plot, simple or complex, which satisfies us and incorpo-
rates their extraordinariness into our own previous sense
of experience. (How could there be a woman like this? How
could there be a runner? How did this man cause a revolution, or small women to faint?) All of our most profound
questions are involved. Each plot is an attempt to answer
them.

Simple structure—beginning, middle, and the end—is
not enough. Neatness does not absolutely count. The man
and what he says, and the exact words he uses, the most
precise note of the styles and contrasts in the properties,
the costumes, the movements into and out of certain levels,
the rhythm itself, counts more: the maker's self in contact
with you, and talking together about the world.

An active play is one in which our view of the situation

changes rapidly. (The same murders, in another play, can remain curiously inert, for all the gunshots.) Activity is more important than mere outline. And with it, a good plot shakes all of us into action.

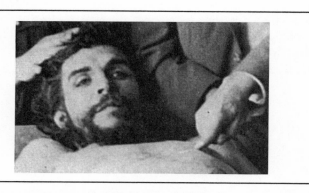

This is not suspense. This is what has already happened. It is over. This plot is a cemetery.

The activity is over: the bodies are left behind as a sign of what went on. In the seconds before their deaths these men no doubt appealed for mercy to their killers. Perhaps there were some glances between their assassin, but the decision had been taken. A rope was tipped, death came. That was it. There was an end to these two men, but the cry comes on over the mob's head to us: we are encountering a lament addressed to our best instincts. And from the acts of the killers, we all hear a threat.

The plot, while active, is a battle for our mind's best sympathy; first we see things one way, then we see them another. We want Henry to win, then his enemy. We want to know how it is going to turn out.

We want to know what the playwright is going to decide. We will listen to the play as his expression, a sign of his life at the time he wrote it. We will never know fully what the author thinks: but the more he knows of his own thoughts, the more we'll be able to read on the page. It is the process by which the playwright gets there that we secretly appreciate the more.

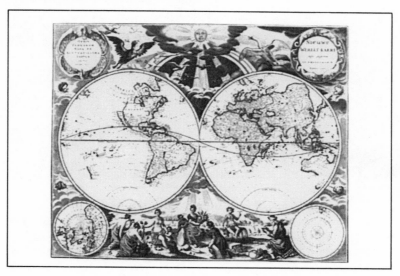

Having moved through it once we make one map.

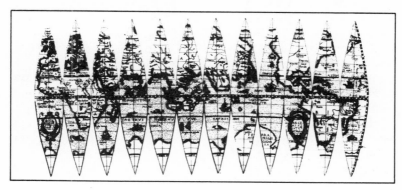

Having moved through it again, we make another. Gradually, we learn the landscape and acquire familiarity with its trees. Gradually, hard truth emerges where prose was felt; gray patches turn pink; the air alters. We find

new sharpness, really, refining our own perceptiveness.

It is useful work carving out frontiers, finding and knowing the land, but even that changes. Each reading, each plow through it changes it a little toward dust, or corn rust, each rain recompacts it, each forest fire. We move through experience. It is our chief activity. It is what can be described as "changing our views," or "learning," or "growing up," or even as "what you do." It is always a battle, and a love affair, and a chase. When it is good, it brings meeting, and some discussions, leading at times to real intercourse. Communication has, and will continue to take place, more or less like the weather: and it will always need a plot to sum up what has already been said moment to moment in the interior of the play.

Each plot is only a temporary vision. The important activity is in the exploring, the developing of still better plots, carrying them forward, making sure they extend into every ravine and corner of the play, then stepping back for a moment, to recognize underneath, that we are moving, mentally, emotionally, physically, the way the playwrights suggested, arguing with them, always adding our own loving variations on their texts.

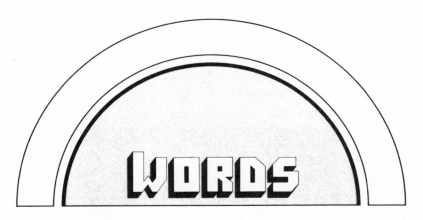

WORDS

ords are images. They are glimpses of the real. In speech, they pour over us, though, like a pattern of sound. Think of the rhymes we used to mumble in grammar schools, the joy we took in matching one sound with another, to make those chants. In the theater, sound flows over us like a river of energies.

As sounds, syllables offer a notation capable of music. One can make symphonies merely of the sounds, as some poets do today.

<pre>
FOREST   FOR
FOR EST   FOR
FOREST   FOREST
FOR
</pre>

LUCKY: *Given the existence as uttered forth in the public works of Puncher and Wattmann of a personal God quaquaquaqua with white beard quaquaquaquaoutside time without extension who from the heights of divine apathia divine athambia divine aphasia loves us dearly with some exceptions for reasons unknown but time will tell. . . .—Waiting for Godot*

Repetition and variation: of vowels, of consonants, of actual rhymes, and of the number of syllables before a given break. These are the drums we have to play with. Commas can interrupt; a period makes a fuller pause; these are but indications of the way we talk, hurrying forward, then coming to a halt.

Before the Renaissance we heard the singing voice behind the words, and the printed text seemed only a hint to the performer. The predominant forms were chants and carols, where the group joined in on the refrain. These meetings, singing together by the fire, or the altar, all had the religious familiarity of the period, and the poems of the Welsh, or the Anglo-Saxons, are as imbued with the spirit as the Old Testament. Poems in time of war, or love, had to work well for groups; they were conceived of, sometimes, as mutual spells.

132

Words give one some power over the world: and double, double, toil and trouble to all who do not understand that fact. Witchery, of course, in part depends on rhythm echoing the self, but accelerating it, like a good dance tune. One can reach ecstasy through rhythm, and words have in our history encouraged such abandoned moments; rising to such a peak, though, one sees the images referred to as well, and one hears a music behind, while the words—as print, as tangible words—dissolve. That is the effect a playwright seeks in the theater.

For words to become invisible, their sound must not intrude too much. Each age has its preference for patterns of sound, and all previous patterns tend to seem ornate to the present generation. Music is not just ornamentation, for through the sound we hear the individual voice, behind, the human one, telling us something of our shared experience.

Some people, like Aeschylus, talk all clotted up in words that come down on us like big logs.

Ah, ah
the rattle of chariots round the city: I hear it.
O Lady Hera,
the groaning axles of the loaded wheels.
Beloved Artemis!
The air is mad with the whirr of spears.
What will happen? our city, what will become of it,
whereto shall the Gods bring an end upon us?

There comes a shower of stones on the top of the battlements!
O beloved Apollo!
There is the rattle of bronze-bound shields at our gates!
—AESCHYLUS, Seven Against Thebes

O then will be charging of plume-waving words with their
*   wild-floating mane,*
And then will be whirling of splinters, and phrases smoothed
*   down with the plane,*
When the man would the grand-stepping maxims, the
*   language gigantic, repel*
Of the hero-creator of thought.
There will his shaggy-born crest upbristle for anger and woe,
Horribly frowning and growling, his fury will launch
*   at the foe,*
Huge-clamped masses of words, with exertion Titanic
*   up-tearing*
Great ship-timber planks for the fray.
—ARISTOPHANES,
commenting on Aeschylus, in The Frogs

The sound suggests something of the way certain people experience life, echoing a military band, or the *Pirates of Penzance*. If you imagine each word spoken as a sword, then say a speech by any author, you will find whether the author prefers to swish, or duel, and how adroitly he does.

Words refer to an entire dictionary of the world. Any reality can be hinted at in words; and beneath even an

abstract word like *justice*, in our minds lie memories of that day at the court, and the principal's office, and the day someone yelled that word at us, when our mind was on something else. Justice: one gets pictures.

Whether they are written out or not, words suggest visual corollaries. And a word-painter like Shakespeare tries in some way to organize the flow of what his words refer to, like a film-maker contemplating a new collage. On the stage or screen, the primary scene is what we see. Words are there, but overhead; they hover like ghosts, and we try to ignore them, to get into the heart of the characters.

Words work on you, will you or no, listen or not—after all, they are in the air. They are part of what you breathe. They affect your view of things, because they remind you of other things. They provoke juxtapositions, new images, odd reminders, other scenes, your own past, your country, the time of the week, the weather, Cambodia. We may be looking at a picture of a nude couple, silently, pleased for their joy.

Then come the words: frontiers: repression. What do the words mean?

They do not mean any one thing. They suggest another frame of reference, something we had not been eager to think about—Puritanism, the French student-labor demonstrations, masked men with helmets breaking skulls open, bars on the windows, and junkies breaking in. Two words, and ten worlds open in the back of our head.

Personal style is reflected first in the choice of content: what subjects does the writer appeal to, what occurs to him? Themes of justice or of injustice, general topics, indicate like the top of an iceberg a solid mass of previous thought; any idea suggests what the author has been thinking about. Particular details: a table of oak, not maple, a dog named Checkers; the word "bopping." These hint even more particularly at the vision being remembered. And then, at the most private, there are those phrases which an author probably does not share with anyone else, secret invented names, codes for a complex of ideas too snarled and personal ever to be fully explicated, names like Blake or Yeats.

Language is sharing: each word represents some general agreement among people who are alive today. We have agreed, for instance, to let the sounds *Ta-ble* stand for that class. A common noun is an agreement among all the people to substitute an image for the thing, so we can talk about it, across distance, without using a moving van.

The dictionary is, in this sense, a list of our agreements, as a people. Start with *sex*, and search it through, and you will find one other thing: the dictionary is a self-consistent set of images. If you do not know about sex before you enter the *s*'s, you will know little more by the time you reach *vagina*, or have passed *penis*; what you will have learned as we all did in grammar school, is an interrelated network of words.

When we know the reality, we let the dictionary go, but perhaps as students of America we should look at words there as our pitiful, but complete, definition of reality. Webster misses what the poets individually see. But he has digested what the people, as a collective "poet," making up the words, have created.

As science has found, there is a limit to definition. Words exist as tools: images, to suggest and hint. It is assumed we know that there are people underneath.

When we look at print, alas, we forget that people ever wrote. Here is where we begin to feel overawed: print has a definiteness about it, and an authority, which make Sunday-schoolers of us all, if we do not watch out. Such suspiciousness makes us back off, and we give up reading. In the theater, though, think of the heyday for the author.

He can refer to a hundred different things a minute, and we in the audience will never see him. He does not have to take individual responsibility. He is a ghost, an inspirer. After all, he seems to say, these are the characters speaking. Not I.

Within a playwright's general style, whether it is rough as O'Neill's, cozy as Coward's, or baroque as John Webster's, we find individual distinctions drawn between the styles of the various characters. If done well enough, these draw our attention away from the author. We want to believe in those people, and if they can just *seem* individuals, we will give them the benefit of the doubt.

How, though, can a playwright make up a character's style? We come again to Nixon. He is the playwright, mocking up a style he thinks appropriate to a Presidential heavyweight. Big words, he says: repetition, and a kind of sing-song chant, and always, a build. So they can give applause.

Let us press toward an open world—a world of open doors, open hearts, open minds—a world open to the reach of the human spirit—a world open in the search for truth and unconcerned with the fate of old dogmas and isms—a world open at last to the light of justice, and the light of reason.
—RICHARD NIXON

His created character seems artificial because the man has cut out the parts that do not "fit." He has not let himself really hit below the belt, where he wants to; he has suggested it, but he has not let himself loose. Control, he thinks—ruining the poetry of it all. Nixon is like any other bad writer: he is so intent on presenting one image of the character, that he allows it no real freedom. Unlike Shakespeare, whose characters are always wandering off into new pastures, Nixon's "character" always talks the same way, or tries to. Consistency is the destroyer.

Imagining, perhaps, is one way we think. Through imagining we can make connections, draw parallels, see resemblances—and draw distinctions, separating like from unlike, shades of difference. And imagining, being a human activity, tends to move toward order, toward a larger synthesis, envisioning a general pattern. We aspire to understanding, and we rise toward it through successive images.

What we focus on, then, becomes essential to the merit of our words. If we look only to the audience, to making *one* impression on them, then that will appear in our words' thinness. If we look at the political only, ignoring the emotions, our words will be out of date as fast as a new nation. As we watch an author's words, images of the real, the playwright prods us into remembering new similarities, and new differences. The better the playwright, the wider and the more particular are these references to material outside the immediate scene, the more he encourages us to encompass in our own imagining. Shakespeare puts in a new way of looking at the scene every line or so.

Shakespeare, from the evidence, takes his plot as given, and makes up excuses for the characters to act the way they do; but instead of "making up" the way a Ben Jonson did, with an apple of observation, and a pound of Latin, all coherence gone, a flurry of unrelated images, a mirage that could hold for an hour or so in an overheated indoor theater, Shakespeare pursues his characters, as if they were already there—after all, he knows their actions beforehand. As he matures he seems to be exploring the characters, allowing them free or random actions at times, just to see what comes up, then returning again and again to certain moral questions which nag at him. Here is Falstaff:

FALSTAFF: *Bardolph, am I not fallen away vilely since this last action? do I not bate? do I not dwindle? Why, my skin hangs about me like an old lady's loose gown; I am withered like an old apple-john. Well, I'll repent, and that suddenly, while I am in some liking; I shall be out of heart shortly, and then I shall have no strength to repent. An I have not forgotten what the inside of a church is made of, I am a peppercorn, a brewer's horse: the inside of a church! Company, villainous company, hath been the spoil of me.*
BARDOLPH: *Sir John, you are so fretful, you cannot live long.*
FALSTAFF: *Why, there is it: come, sing me a bawdy song; make me merry. I was as virtuously given as a gentleman need to be; virtuous enough; swore little; diced not above seven times a week; went to a bawdy-house not above once in a quarter—of an hour; paid money that I borrowed, three or four times; lived well, and in good compass: and now I live out of all order, out of all compass.*
BARDOLPH: *Why, you are so fat, Sir John, that you must needs be out of all compass; out of all reasonable compass, Sir John.—I Henry IV*

What a range of sounds, what a range of visions, and worlds referred to. The speech is rich in its language, perhaps because Shakespeare was focusing on the characters and their relationships. But think of what it reminds him of: he begins writing knowing he is going to have them in a tavern. The scene reminds him of fat, and skin, and an old lady's loose gown, an old apple; it reminds him of the moral problems, repentance, and then, just "liking." Shapespeare, it seems, goes where he likes, into the inside of a church, then to a brewer's horse.

The ordering of all this range is first within the character; it is modulated to the character; then to the scene; then to the play as a whole, where a brewer's horse comes to be seen as a particular example of a tendency to think a lot about drinking, and its related subjects. Then we come to Shakespeare himself. He is almost anonymous, having allowed his imagination such free play.

Unlike Nixon's, Shakespeare's style is beyond definition—less personally revealing on the surface than any since Ovid, but always hinting at the way he experiences things. Style is the way one writes: but that involves, as its component drives, the way one thinks, the way one lives, the way one experiences emotions—how one perceives, moving through real life. The individual soul, again. Words are signs of how we live, inside, as much or more than our shoes.

Shakespeare seems to have trusted that through imagination all would come together in the end. Perhaps he is right. Perhaps that is the only way the world could get together, as a coherent vision—on stage, where the words themselves shape events, without intruding, reminding us repeatedly of subjects, visions, glimpses that Shakespeare himself wanted us to be reminded of, leading us, as rapidly as possible, through an exploration of his own mind, contemplating Falstaff, or putting his own compass around the globe.

Enter THESEUS, HIPPOLYTA, PHILOSTRATE,
LORDS, and ATTENDANTS
HIPPOLYTA: *'Tis strange, my Theseus, that these lovers*
speak of.
THESEUS: *More strange than true: I never may believe*
These antique fables, nor these fairy toys.
Lovers and madmen have such seething brains,
Such shaping fantasies, that apprehend
More than cool reason ever comprehends.
The lunatic, the lover and the poet
Are of imagination all compact:
One sees more devils than vast hell can hold;
That is, the madman: the lover, all as frantic,
Sees Helen's beauty in a brow of Egypt:
The poet's eye, in a fine frenzy rolling,
Doth glance from heaven to earth, from earth to heaven;
And as imagination bodies forth
The forms of things unknown, the poet's pen
Turns them to shapes, and gives to airy nothing
A local habitation and a name.
Such tricks hath strong imagination,
That if it would but apprehend some joy,
It comprehends some bringer of that joy;
Or in the night, imagining some fear,
How easy is a bush supposed a bear!
HIPPOLYTA: *But all the story of the night told over,*
And all their minds transfigured so together,
More witnesseth than fancy's images,
And grows to something of great constancy;
But howsoever, strange and admirable.
—A Midsummer-Night's Dream

CHAR-ACTERS

In the old religion, the religion of Puck, and the little people, druids made images of people. A pin in the head of a doll, they felt, could work some headache on the person whose old dress they had placed around the clay.

Images of people, characters, and images of the world, words, were the subject of religious contemplation, as well: one reflected on them, explored their meaning, sensed, fumbled. Logic was not at question here. It was a matter of imagining.

Divining the truth? In part. But more, setting up images to be examined, pictures and statues—but think how much more modern it would be, in the time Shakespeare was writing, to have real people on stage, talking of nature, and fortune, and the other pagan divinities, within a Christian context. Puck leaps up at the moment when the old religion had finally gone under for good, talking of art, not religion.

Imagine trying to describe one of our leaders. We can bring to bear all the questions of anthropology—of class, status, cultural background, age, financial and political power, prejudice, and opinion—and still not know exactly where he or she stands. This is not to say we should give up: we should, actually, ask many more of these questions, realizing all the time how impossible it is to find one word, or one phrase, that can sum up a person. "That bastard," "That bitch," these say a lot, and only a little. Our reaction, really, not a character portrait, is all we ever come out of such investigations with. We like or do not like, we admire, we are drawn into fears, and into conceptions of empire, as we contemplate any prominent character.

Imaging, thus, is a test of how sensitive we are to people, in life. What do you associate, what springs to mind, what occurs to you, along a given plotline; what topics strike you as somehow of relevance—follow them, explore the entire forest of your mind, for whatever strikes you.

The Romans set up statues of their Emperors as gods

for the common folk. Every crossroads had one. Where the three roads come together, went the saying, there will be the image of the Emperor. Augustus, the first one, scoffed at the idea, but allowed it; the rest of them employed it for political purposes. Such images, at the *tres viae*, became trivial. Underneath, of course, the stone sometimes said the man's name, followed by S.P.Q.R.: the phrase was borrowed from the days of Republic, when citizens had a chance to vote, and Rome was truly the Senate and the People of Rome.

Senatus Populus Que Romanus: an idea of a citizen, in a state, embodied in an image of a man. What character speaks out to us, though, across the Dark Ages?

In even thinking about another person's "character," we are performing the act of a playwright, imagining. And we have something in common with Shakespeare, as he created Falstaff, or King Lear. We canvass our own past experience, and what we know from books for parallels, for contrasts, moving always toward a more precise definition, while at the same time allowing as much complication as we have time for. After all, the speed of movement of imagining is what puts Shakespeare out in front of most of us; going from heaven to earth, from earth to heaven, for examples, his imagination, as Puck says in *A Midsummer-Night's Dream,* "puts a girdle round about the earth in forty minutes."

A character like Falstaff is so rich, and so complex, that we may pursue the question, "What was he like?" almost endlessly, investigating every cranny of the play for indications of Shakespeare's attitude toward honor, or drinking, then bringing it back, and judging Falstaff. Shakespeare's plays, like life, encourage judgment.

Imagining is one way we think. As we watch a character, sometimes like him, sometimes unlike, metaphorically, moving backward and forward, struggling for a unified view the playwright prods us into remembering new problems, new pasts, new arguments. Range brings depth; the better the playwright the wider and the more particular are these references outward, the more he encourages us to encompass, in our imagining. Perhaps character is, after all is said and done, persistence of image.

Innocently falling under Shakespeare's complex spell, nineteenth-century critics tried to answer the mysteries of character which an ambitious quiet man like Macbeth can raise when he captures one's imagination. They were not utterly wrong. Shakespeare, after all, had encouraged them to think about such questions, even if he had also—line by line—made sure no one answer would be sufficient.

Falstaff is a coward, some said; Falstaff is a heroic battler against false ideals of honor; Falstaff is a drunk; Falstaff is a threat to the young prince, who corrupts himself by sharing a tavern room, and perhaps even a whore, with such thieving companions; Falstaff is a memory of some man Shakespeare may have known in Stratford. Listening to such comments from his posthumous audience. Shakespeare's ghost surely smiles, with the Mona Lisa wink he

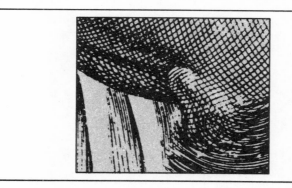

has in the Chandos portrait, for a moment's reflection on Falstaff can show us that all these statements are true, and all are in some way an effort to get over the effect of the character, to place Falstaff, and yet all, failing to pinion him with one phrase, fall back to re-examining the play. Re-examining is part of the point—it is like contemplation.

Falstaff is not a person: he is an image of a person,

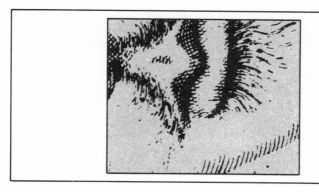

probably a composite of a number of people, seen at a hundred different hours on days as different as rain and sleet, and in taverns. Contemplating an image of a person involves us in the questions which the Renaissance felt important: humor, psychology, morality, and even love. And such questions always have at least two sides.

For Aristotle, it seems, character is whatever we most generally persist in doing, a habit of action. Real moral decisions gradually get added up in our minds to some pattern—just as in the street we add up the blue work shirt, the blue jeans, the green paint on the shoes, and decide, this woman is a painter. All actions can be viewed as moral—in some aspect they suggest or affect our relationships with others—even the wearing of a work shirt, in the context of a given culture, suggests several moral choices the person may have made.

Only action will really tell, we think. We watch the person, judging. Borrowing an idea from Aeschylus, Aristotle suggests that the audience is like a jury deciding whether or not a killer is pure, or so impious as to deserve to be stoned to death. Oedipus Rex killed his father and slept with his mother: take it to the jury. Let the people decide.

If we feel that we could have made the same mistakes, we begin to feel pity for that character; and if we feel that the person's sufferings could happen to us as well, we may also begin to feel fear—and with that identification the tragic figure is acquitted.

The character goes free in minds—persists as an image, puzzles, encourages us to reconsider the whole play again, from every moral angle the author suggests, and more. After examining the whole we may come again to some judgment, about Oedipus, and about ourselves. Emerging from the confusion of claim and counterclaim, from law and forgiveness, from decisions about the way in which the character is like us, and different from us, we realize we have been imagining.

Like a candle, the image of a character has an afterglow, a strange persistence. We move toward it, trying to be more clear, to express it—and like a will-o'-the-wisp, it retreats. This fire in the swamps was thought to be like a spirit, who hovered near the edge to draw people in.

Clearly persistence is not all. Bad plays have such consistent characters that we predict their every line. This leads to boredom.

Complexity comes from the range of things the playwright is reminded of, moment to moment, describing, or sketching the character. Hazlitt says in some amazement of Shakespeare: "He brings together images the most alike, but placed at the greatest distance from each other; that is, found in circumstances of the greatest dissimilitude." Shakespeare's mind ranges all over, and he comes back with hundreds of parallels, from earlier books, from life's multiple experiences, to stories he has heard about only at the tavern, referring from Falstaff to knighthood, old judges, drunks, and boasters. Thus we are reminded of a number of other moments, and each moment we are reminded of, each vision provides us with another handle by which we can see the scene he has in mind.

Hazlitt argues, "The poet may be said, for the time, to identify himself with the character he wishes to represent, and to pass from one to another, like the same soul successively animating different bodies." What good training, for a soul! If one could transmigrate so easily, no Hindu would ever have to return, lifetime after lifetime, working his way up from a flower to a human, and beyond. Why, it is as if one could live entirely free from one's own personality, and place, could fly through every soul, visiting even Helen of Troy, or the Pope. If Shakespeare ransacked his memory to make Falstaff, think of how many people he mentally revisited, trying somehow to sense their essential spirit, in an exact moment.

Cohesion is in the eye of the beholder: first, in the mind of the playwright, as he sees some parallel between a thousand different instances of life—yet retaining the distinctness of each, so each may work distinctly, on our imaginations. Shakespeare opposed obliterating divergence of views, knocking off the edges until the character seemed only an ideal type. But, pursuing some unity of conception of his own, he dovetails his distinctions so that they all seem, somehow, to work together. He creates a mystery, and suggests that the answer to our perplexed questions about how the character's moments all fit together may be found a little later on.

HOTSPUR: *My liege, I did deny no prisoners.*
But I remember, when the fight was done,
When I was dry with rage and extreme toil,
Breathless and faint, leaning upon my sword,
Came there a certain lord, neat, trimly dress'd,
Fresh as a bridegroom; and his chin new reap'd
Show'd like a stubble-land at harvest-home.
He was perfumed like a milliner;
And 'twixt his finger and his thumb he held
A pouncet-box, which ever and anon
He gave his nose and took 't away again;
Who therewith angry, when it next came there,
Took it in snuff; and still he smiled and talk'd,
And as the soldiers bore dead bodies by,
He call'd them untaught knaves, unmannerly,
To bring a slovenly unhandsome corse
Betwixt' the wind and his nobility.
With many holiday and lady terms
He question'd me; amongst the rest, demanded
My prisoners in your majesty's behalf.
I then, all smarting with my wounds being cold,
To be so pester'd with a popinjay,
Out of my grief and my impatience,

Answer'd neglectingly I know not what,
He should, or he should not; for he made me mad
To see him shine so brisk, and smell so sweet,
And talk so like a waiting-gentlewoman
Of guns and drums and wounds,—God save the mark!—
And telling me the sovereign'st thing on earth
Was parmaceti for an inward bruise;
And that it was great pity, so it was,
This villainous salt-petre should be digg'd
Out of the bowels of the harmless earth,
Which many a good tall fellow had destroy'd
So cowardly; and but for these vile guns,
He would himself have been a soldier.

This bald unjointed chat of his, my lord,
I answered indirectly, as I said;
And I beseech you, let not his report
Come current for an accusation
Betwixt my love and your high majesty.
—I Henry IV

Note how the eye shifts: we see the dress, then we get a comparison, "fresh as a bridegroom." We are kicked out of the base situation to another, and the contrast makes the perfumed lord ridiculous. He is out of place in a battlefield, and his every instinct insists upon it. He is shaved, and holds his snuff too delicately, while the soldiers bring dead bodies by.

Then the lord outdoes himself, going one better than mere affectation. He seems so dainty and so sensitive that he accuses the soldiers of being boorish, to bring corpses near him. They are untaught; unmannerly; and corpses are smelly, "Unhandsome," "slovenly." This lord, we may say, takes the aesthetic view.

He would seem to have been born on perfume, and bred without hard work. He is insulted that the very smell of death should come "betwixt the wind and his nobility." The images pile up.

We sense Shakespeare's own attitude (though we do not know it). And think of all the directions he goes in, describing the scene—first looking at the real situation itself, with the smoke clearing; then describing the lord; then recalling parallels from a whole courtly world; then, remembering who is supposed to be talking, talking in the style of Hotspur, who is, in the actual situation, talking to the king. We sympathize, with Hotspur on the spot, but right now the King demands the prisoners. This Hotspur will not do. His impulsive refusal of the battlefield becomes congealed in a stubbornness that will cause war.

Our view of the character slides from one framework to another: multiple angles. Like Plutarch, Shakespeare enjoys considering a character from all possible sides—or, at least, from whatever ones that occur to him.

That courtier is made up: but he is made up of so many

realistic observations, all more or less of the same kind of person that he has more life than a real courtier might. More life? More life on stage, more life in art. That is, he has more image per square inch, more suggestion. And why? Not from an accumulation of detail, the crutches of a weak writer, but from the very intensity with which Shakespeare examines every aspect of the character—as if he were pursuing the "heart" of a character. His effort to find the core of Lear is infectious. His own pursuits encourage us to try the same thing.

And as we move through such considerings, the character appears to grow before our very eyes. The character takes on a life of his own, becomes visible. Put that character up on stage, and our minds are drawn in so many different tasty directions, we almost ignore the author. We like to: we want to watch the people. We want to believe.

Like most people, most authors try to convince you they are right about a given character. Shakespeare knows they are made up, and just goes on to play, selecting real moments from a number of people, writing them in under one character's name, letting the audience put it together—the way they like it best.

Most authors make up their own plots, to say something. Shakespeare seized on the plot as if it were true, and as an image of some emotional and philosophic quarrel; and instead of "describing the truth," he explored. The tentativeness makes for progression in the plays. His characters grow, on stage. Ben Jonson, one senses within a few lines, has the whole mystery clear in his head before he writes, and as a result his tragedies die before the speech by Cicero is half through: cold, diagrammatic, moral. His plays are the ones that critics remake Shakespeare's into, when they imply that before writing *Hamlet* he had worked out a philosophic text of some three hundred pages, all to be transferred point by point into line by line of a moving character's speech, while he jumps in and out of a grave.

Immortality in a work of art was something the Renaissance always dreamed of: and perhaps Shakespeare had seen that the morality plays of his youth, so earnest, and so definite, so clear in their conclusions, left one with only smoke, explosions, and a longing for the devil to come back. Enigmas, conflicts, these aroused interest—and kept it alive after the play—particularly if in the broader lines, the character strode like a colossus through all obstacles. What fun to make a drunk, the old morality figure of evil, into the most attractive, the most educated, the most courtly, the most debauched, and the friendliest character in a play.

Playing gets one further than philosophy, though both

are complementary: and characters make the best images, stir the imagination most, and longest. They are *like* people. All images involve the primal *as if*. Shakespeare's characters are as if immortal, they have lived so long.

Imagining, dreaming, loving, and writing poetry: they are all crazy, Shakespeare said, indulging, it seems, in all of them in his plays. Under the old religion, before Saint Patrick brought a veneer of Christianity into Britain, faeries were prominent, and druids like those in Wales and Stonehenge created images for their people to consider on, wells which reminded one of grace, corn dolls which spoke of renewed fertility, poems which were runes. The old style (carried on in Christian meditation) was the cryptic: knowledge encased in riddles, sacred because it was devoted to an expression of the more mystical truths of their day, but holding off the common touch from assuming too easily that "they understood." Shakespeare writes of individual people, where the old folks talked of gods.

TOTALITY

tonehenge is a circle of stones set on a slight hill. Druids used the place for their rites, aligning themselves with the sun and the moon at the astrological peaks of their lives; priests of the new religion, Christianity, inveighed against it; sculptors in the twentieth century have gone to those great heavy stones for models, rediscovering the sophistication of the primitive. Who is to say what Stonehenge is?

How can one sum up a thing without taking into account the rest of the universe? One can only say what it feels like, now, including everything we know, all at once, at the intersection of time we happen to be in, with all of our personal biases showing, so others will know how to accord or reject. We must assume that our personality is where it all comes together.

Each of us is irradiated by life. A play tries to sum up some aspects of life; to offer them for contemplation, and to enlist our imaginations in the mutual effort which we call an evening in the theater. When we go, we are listening through all the speeches for some voice behind. Afterward, though, how can we sum it all up?

The totality is what we exchange. A work may have a verbal unity, and still be inactive, because its author somehow never manages to hit on topics that we care about. *The Rape of the Lock*, for instance, for all its satiric play, strikes some people as a long poem about a trivial social event, the taking of a small lock of hair. Triviality will always out: that is the motto of time. Depth may show: or it may be killed. The druids no longer have a really continuous tradition—that having been viciously smashed over the last few centuries—their stones stand mute, if enigmatic.

Shakespeare's plays are the main relic from his culture which people in America know. Few read Francis Bacon; fewer still Sir Walter Raleigh's *History of the World.* Shakespeare, in our schools, occupies the position of the Bible: the strongest authority, in the realm of play, reduced to a text for tenth graders. Queen Elizabeth I herself is a footnote.

When we first look at a play, we tend to see what is up front: the words, the characters, the black costume Hamlet is wearing. But, in the conflict of the styles involved, we can begin to hear the playwright, pondering; it is as if through Hamlet Shakespeare's ghost could talk to us. This is not just poetry: it is a communication, across vast amounts of time and miles, from one person, through others, to us. The totality is, then, in the exchange.

Like a circle of stones, a structure of words can form a complete ring, being as unified within itself as a set of Henry Vaughan's poems, or as regular as Plato. But if there is insufficient conflict visible in the work, we will find no entry.

We enter any field of knowledge through the holes. It is a technique of scholarship. One studies everything that is known, noting the unresolved conflicts; if one is to bring the field forward, one concentrates on the gaps. Through those gaps one finds the new understanding.

Shakespeare's plays have more conflict than most, and hence, more means of entry. What does he mean, Hamlet is delaying? What is Lear doing out on the heath? Questions, enigmas, all accompanied by such strength and force of plot, such apparently simple actions, moment to moment, that the whole, we think, must surely mean one thing. It probably means more.

Try to imagine the playwright at work. Auden says:

How can I know what I think till I see what I say? A poet writes "The chestnut's comfortable root," and then changes this to "The chestnut's customary root." In this alteration there is no question of replacing one emotion by another, or of strengthening an emotion, but of discovering what the emotion is. The emotion is unchanged, but waiting to be identified like a telephone number one cannot remember.

Never forget that play-making is a process: it goes on, and it is a process of discovering. One has the feeling, and attempts to clarify it; to express it, by drawing parallels; to communicate exactly how it feels. All the techniques of literature are but attempts to regularize the paths.

Here is the first scene from Shakespeare's last play. Try following the movement of his mind, as he wrote it, line by line. What we have here before us is a printed version more or less like what he had on the foolscap, after he finished writing the scene.

On a ship at sea:
A tempestuous noise of thunder and lightning heard
Enter a SHIPMASTER and a BOATSWAIN
MASTER: *Boatswain!*
BOATSWAIN: *Here, master: what cheer?*
MASTER: *Good; speak to the mariners: fall to't yarely, or we run ourselves aground: bestir, bestir.* (Exit)
(Enter MARINERS)
BOATSWAIN: *Heigh, my hearts! cheerly, cheerly, my hearts! yare, yare! Take in the topsail. Tend to the master's whistle. Blow, till thou burst thy wind, if room enough!*
(Enter ALONSO, SEBASTIAN, ANTONIO, FERDINAND, GONZALO, and others)

ALONSO: *Good boatswain, have care. Where's the master? Play the men.*
BOATSWAIN: *I pray now, keep below.*
ANTONIO: *Where is the master, boatswain?*
BOATSWAIN: *Do you not hear him? You mar our labour: keep your cabins: you do assist the storm.*
GONZALO: *Nay, good, be patient.*
BOATSWAIN: *When the sea is. Hence! What cares these roarers for the name of king? To cabin: silence! trouble us not.*
GONZALO: *Good, yet remember whom thou hast aboard.*
BOATSWAIN: *None that I more love than myself. You are a counsellor; if you can command these elements to silence, and work the peace of the present, we will not hand a rope more; use your authority: if you cannot, give thanks you have lived so long, and make yourself ready in your cabin for the mischance of the hour, if it so hap. Cheerly, good hearts! Out of our way, I say.* (Exit)
GONZALO: *I have great comfort from this fellow: methinks he hath no drowning mark upon him; his complexion is perfect gallows. Stand fast, good Fate, to his hanging: make the rope of his destiny our cable, for our own doth little advantage. If he be not born to be hanged, our case is miserable.* (Exeunt)
(Re-enter BOATSWAIN)
BOATSWAIN: *Down with the topmast! yare! lower, lower! Bring her to try with main-course.* (A cry within) *A plague upon this howling! They are louder than the weather or our office.* (Re-enter SEBASTIAN, ANTONIO, and GONZALO) *Yet again! What do you here? Shall we give o'er, and drown? Have you a mind to sink?*
SEBASTIAN: *A pox o' your throat, you bawling, blasphemous, incharitable dog!*
BOATSWAIN: *Work you, then.*
ANTONIO: *Hang, cur! hang you whoreson, insolent noisemaker. We are less afraid to be drowned than thou art.*
GONZALO: *I'll warrant him for drowning; though the ship were no stronger than a nutshell, and as leaky as an unstanched wench.*
BOATSWAIN: *Lay her a-hold, a-hold! set her two courses off to sea again; lay her off.*
(Enter MARINERS wet)
MARINERS: *All lost! to prayers, to prayers! all lost!*
BOATSWAIN: *What, must our mouths be cold?*
GONZALO: *The king and prince at prayers! let's assist them, For our case is as theirs.*
SEBASTIAN: *I'm out of patience.*
ANTONIO: *We are merely cheated of our lives by drunkards: This wide-chapp'd rascal,—would thou mightst lie drowning The washing of ten tides!*
GONZALO: *He'll be hang'd yet, Though every drop of water swear against it,*

And gape at wid'st to glut him.
> (A confused noise within:
> *"Mercy on us!"*—
"We split, we split!"—*"Farewell, my wife and children!*—
Farewell, brother!"—*"We split, we split, we split!"*)
ANTONIO: *Let's all sink with the king.*
SEBASTIAN: *Let's take leave of him.*
> (Exeunt ANTONIO and SEBASTIAN)
GONZALO: *Now would I give a thousand furlongs of sea
for an acre of barren ground, long heath, brown furze,
anything. The wills above be done; but I would fain die a
dry death.* (Exeunt)—*The Tempest*

The gestures are frenetic. The sailors are trying to keep
the sails from hauling the boat aground, pulling down
against the stretched belly of the canvas. The courtiers are
interfering, talking in the space the sailors need to work.
"Out of our way," the boatswain says, knowing it is an
emergency. And the courtiers snarl some more. The sailors
try to lower the top mast, and to bring the helm around,
back to the main course. Then the mariners come in wet,
crying "All lost! to prayers, to prayers! all lost!" The
courtiers complain some more, until the confused noise
within strikes even them: the boat is splitting open. "Let's
all sink with the king," says Antonio, ever noble. The more
human Sebastian, or at least, the commoner in him, speaks
quickly, "Let's take leave of him," and they exit.

A maze of chaotic movement: a veritable storm itself,
the style of gesture here. Costuming, by contrast, is
hardly stressed: the mariners come in wet: the clothes,
though obviously distinguishing the mariners from the more
elegant courtiers, are of secondary importance in Shakespeare's mind here. He hardly pauses to make much point
with them, nor with hand properties. Again, the implication is, this is too extreme a situation for such amenities.

The setting, then, breaks open: we are in a theater, and
though there may be a backdrop, it is clear that we are
imagining the stage as a ship, with the actors bucking and
tossing, perhaps, to suggest the rolls, under waves from
the side. There may well have been some suggestion in
production, a railing, or a net of rigging, but there are no
such "complete battleship with 16-inch guns" as we find in
ninteenth-century productions. This is only a hint. In back,
there are doors which go "within"—within being, really,
into the backstage area. These doors hint that the rest of the
theater is the invisible ship itself.

We are all on board. Water and wind are the largest
part of the invisible setting, splashing from buckets, perhaps, and making the mariners' clothes wet—and on the

stage, we have a portion of the deck. By not showing it all on stage, by talking of such a storm, Shakespeare suggests that it is all around his audience. The style of setting is baroque: a few lurid examples, and certain words. His focus is on the characters more than on the storm itself.

The words, which in the theater we would hear mainly as shouts, and complaints, are full of questions and exclamations, jerks, uncompleted thoughts. Shakespeare comes at us like his spirit Ariel, prodding us with every new word—Yare, Yare. The general style of the scene suggests trouble.

And as we look at the way the language of the characters is distinguished, as we look at their individual styles, we see the class distinction opening up. The sailors tend to talk one word at a time: "Heigh, my hearts! cheerly, cheerly, my hearts! yare, yare!" Long sentences are for courtiers.

The characters, then, are temporarily distinguished by class. Master speaks to boatswain, boatswain speaks to the mariners; courtiers, representing the king, bellow at the boatswain—the master of the ship having gone off stage after the fifth line. The ship is left to the middle men. And in such a storm, the natural impulse of people to save themselves, no matter what their status, comes to the surface.

Shakespeare has raised a storm so large that people are thrown back upon themselves; as individuals, they clash, while the king sits below, out of sight, praying. They all imagine, at least for a moment, abandoning him for any stretch of dry land they could get.

Shakespeare has set up a situation in which he himself is like the storm, driving these people to their own extremes: it is a scene of rage and prayer. The plot is chaos, followed by splitting: the end, we gather, is the sinking of the ship. Cut. The next scene, we find the daughter of the magician who has raised this storm; she is talking of the effects it had on her, suggesting, at least partially, the effects Shakespeare hoped to evoke.

MIRANDA: *If by your art, my dearest father, you have*
Put the wild waters in this roar, allay them.
The sky, it seems, would pour down stinking pitch,
But that the sea, mounting to the welkin's cheek,
Dashes the fire out. O, I have suffer'd
With those that I saw suffer! a brave vessel,
Who had, no doubt, some noble creature in her,
Dash'd all to pieces. O, the cry did knock
Against my very heart! Poor souls, they perish'd.
Had I been any god of power, I would
Have sunk the sea within the earth, or ere
It should the good ship so have swallow'd and
The fraughting souls within her. —The Tempest

His prime concern is with the souls on board. As he follows them, moment to moment, in the actual scene, we notice that he skimps on discussion of costume and properties (the style of these is crude, where he mentions them at all), focusing in on gesture, sound, action, and character, shaping the whole with his words, the breezes that make the scene itself. But the style of gesture is explosive, and complex, full of real elbows, and shoves: whereas the style of setting, though referring to a violent natural phenomenon, shows us little more than a stage and some rigging—it is far more suggestive than demonstrative. There is, then, a choice here: to point up certain elements in the scene, and to leave the ocean off stage.

Action may be what we are reduced to in an emergency: but Shakespeare's people will always have a few words, to comment—and, therefore, affect the way we view what is going on. The references outward are to the state, and to society—to conflicts, hangings, powers, blasphemy, charity; to being cheated of our lives. There is the larger setting, in Shakespeare's mind. And so, knowing the old comparison of the ship to the state, we may be forgiven if we come away feeling that the question Shakespeare has asked himself, at some point before writing this scene, is: What do you do when your society seems to be falling apart? "We split, we split."

Miranda has no answer except to turn to her father, the man who made the tempest. Such storms, it seems, are educational: and Prospero, like an artist, shows people in trouble without actually breaking their skulls. He affects the world, but unlike a politician, his small mistakes do not kill. We are beginning to turn from the state to the artist, reflecting on what it means to show the world in small.

To find the personality in process, look to the conflicts. It is clear that what we have is the coherence of a man thinking along certain lines, on certain dominating conflicts, on certain forebodings, trying in some way, in the scene, to sum it all up, to provide a metaphor for the conflicts inside. That does not mean he finds an answer. In fact, the scene suggests he will explore the conflicts more, on drier ground, hoping for a solution, but fearing the worst, about the state. It is Shakespeare foreseeing the dissolution of his culture. He saw here such a storm that kings would hide below, and their courtiers would lord it over the middle men, the men who actually ran the ships, driving them to bitter opposition, as the ship itself split. What then? The future was as obscure as a tempest at sea.

Whether we are dealing with Nixon, our landlord, or our

neighbor, making up any kind of a play, each of these is a language: settings, properties, costumes, gestures, plots, characters, and words themselves. And each can be manipulated by a playwright in his own way. And usually the style of setting will differ markedly from the style of words—suggesting the conflict within the playwright's own mind.

How does it all fit together? The answer is: in the personality of the playwright. And nowhere else? Well, we can each rederive from each of his references some vision of the world, and we can call that the author's, but it is really our own. Some criticism interacts fully with the author, some does not: but it is all fiction.

Anything we say about a work of art is fiction: our personal biases speak through our very misinterpretations. In fiction, as in criticism, one should try to tell the truth. But more, once we realize that what we are writing is always an abstract kind of a novel, we should learn to respect the demand that we make art.

Art is magic. It brings us revelations, recognitions, moments of discovery. It changes our view of the universe, only to bring us back to ourselves, mysteriously enlarged. With art our eyes grow bigger.

In considering any play, we should stay aware of the distinctness of each different style, while trying to follow the playwright's mind at work, as he moves among them. The questions of value are those we would ask about anyone's movement of mind: how fast? How deep? How broad? How new—that is, how original?

With that, of course, we begin to ask how much of his own perceptions he actually allows out, on the paper. (Lack of originality is actually the result of great labor, knocking off all one's own perceptions to fit into the uniform our eighth-grade teachers sewed up for us. Typical are business letters.) Shakespeare seems to have let a great many of his own "moments of perception" slip into the speech Hotspur gives, or Falstaff's dialogue. Why not follow his good example?

In thinking about a play, we are considering the playwright underneath, and beyond a judgment on his mind, our own heart asks: what conflicts is he focusing on most? Congreve looks to the clothes and the manners, and divides the world into foreground and a gossiping group in the background, moving toward a dance at the end. The conflicts he attends to are qualitatively different from those of Wycherly, who is more interested in sex than society, and consequently a bit more bitter in his views. Each playwright devotes most time to several particular languages, ranking them varyingly in importance, depending on the tone he wants to set in the image he puts onstage. Any real play is a conflict of styles: and the way through it is on the trail of the movement of the playwright's mind, presenting the play to us. We all dream of tracking someone down, and a bad playwright can be found out: a good one is so openly mysterious that there is no bottom, no single "point." In a good play, following, pursuing, is the only point, imagining, moment to moment. Is not imagining enough?

To describe such an activity, of course, would take a novel of at least five hundred pages, just for *Hamlet*. It could involve a consideration of the entire culture of Renaissance England—all the possible inputs. It would involve all we know about Shakespeare, and what we think he meant by each word. It would involve more: our own honest reaction, after such study, to each line as the pattern of the meaning changes before our eyes. Henry James might be a good ghost, for such a work, or Norman Mailer, stoned. To come close to "what he meant" one almost creates a biography and, to be fully honest, one should distinguish one's own reactions—as someone from the present, reacting—so that a reader of our critique might gain entry to Shakespeare through our own era's attitudes as well. Well, it is a big book.

What most critics do today is small stuff, even if scholarly. None of us wants to write vast tomes. Write it short, and you will have a fiction. Charles and Mary Lamb called their version *Tales from Shakespeare*.

One should know everything—a simple desire. But failing that, and looking for a shorter way to digest it all, and say as much as we can about a given problem, make a play. We do it with our lives.

Comparing, contrasting, checking past against present, act against word, watching each language in turn, imagining through all the categories, we acquaint our minds with a playwright's character, even if we come to few hard conclusions: most of our mental reviews are mixed. Allow the mix while you search, and you will end up absorbing more data; then, after a little play, a new answer will come. It will not be words, necessarily—remember your own self—it will be a new way of acting, for yourself, in this field.

What succeeds, what fails, what is best, what is worst, these are the arguments of any play—in the ball park, or in the restaurant, wherever people put on scenes, act out, and re-create the world, explaining that their grandfather said, and then the neighbor said, "And do you want some salt?" Everywhere we walk, someone is suffering, in the distance; their lives reflect our own.

This play is a kind of faith. Each person is, at a human

level, alike. Humanity is where we come together.

Thinking a little more about others might help them, but instead of being a burden, make it play. On the subway, depressed arms reaching up, most people look at the floor. Look up. Look in someone else's eyes. After all, we would all *like* to be together; we are just painfully aware of being apart, distanced from other human beings, and that depresses us, keeps us from looking up. Who knows what crazy person may be looking back?

But if you do it just for fun, where is the harm? And who knows, you might see something. How else does love begin?

It seems to be our nature to call out across the ocean to each other. This, finally, is the end, the round, the closure of play. The ring, beginning with our own building, our desk, even, proceeding out into the world, to the particular playwright, to the multiplicity of playwrights in our governments—to the world's complex setting, properties, costume, gesture, and ignorance—climbing, then, through reflection on the whole, into some more sufficient knowledge of itself, by itself, creating and reassembling, as it grows into culture after culture—as another playwright sees it coming by, and describes it, once, and then again, the culture changing as the playwright acts on it, the ring in which

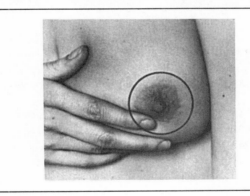

you become as much of yourself as you can, becoming gold or steel, depending on our own natures—a secret—Dionysus's own—playing leading into loving, and loving, through experience, to a more thorough intercourse, and that, playing more, leading at times to ecstasy.

Such a lust is natural, as well; known deeply enough we are each other. In that spirit, then, approach all plays, pick what is interesting, and begin there, reflecting, considering—it is arguing with yourself, and remember: the world is who we are.

This show has brought a brief review of the elements of play, a brief anatomy of playwrights, and thoughts, play within play, and if unusual in shape, why imagine it merely as a prayer book for Dionysus, or the world, and all may be easier.

And in the end, remember what all play may say: Dionysus speaks to you: make life into its own show, transform the world, and bring on the outrageous harmonious feast, Thanksgiving.

RE·CREA·TIONS

The play always brings us back to society. The same detailed analysis which clarifies the stage art can make sense of life scenes. Theater—along with sports, camping, travel—is mixed together under the umbrella term "recreation," which is synonymous with "exercise," "doing things." But play's function is much deeper than leisure; play is a kind of public dreaming. In a secular society, play becomes one of the few important symbol-giving ceremonies. Mircea Eliade has pointed out:

The symbol not only makes the world "open" but also helps religious man to attain the universal. For it is through symbols that man finds his way out of his particular situation and "opens himself" to the general and the universal. Symbols awaken individual experience and transmute it into a spiritual act, into metaphysical comprehension of the world.—The Sacred and the Profane

Although on stage, some theater wants to reproduce the world as precisely as the child wants to reproduce home life by "playing house," play at its most delightful and profound is never "realistic."

Whether on stage or in a stadium, the area set aside for playing is special. We call it a *"play*ground." The space is symbolically sacred. The player and the spectator are both "taken out of themselves"; that is, the very act of playing re-creates a universe outside Time and historical place. Re-creation is a means of symbolically starting afresh.

In primitive societies, the sacredness we associate with child's play—that ability to see objects both as themselves and as signs of some higher order—is the central reality of the society.

The religious festival is the reactualization of a primordial event, of a sacred history in which the actors are the gods or semi-divine beings. But sacred history is recounted in the myths. Hence the participants in the festival become contemporaries of the gods and semi-divine beings. They live in the primordial time that is sanctified by the gods.—The Sacred and the Profane

The idea of a people *living the universal* is nostalgic to technological man. He is often awed by the child's capacity for wonder, it's ability to feel the spiritual in everyday; but even the adult attempts symbolic acts of renewal in his play.

Modern man's private mythologies—his dreams, reveries, fantasies, and so on—never rise to the ontological status of myths, precisely because they are not experienced by the whole man *and therefore do not transform a particular situation into a situation that is paradigmatic.*
—The Sacred and the Profane

Nevertheless, modern man's spiritual yearning is real; and its vestige is exhibited in many different kinds of performances. People follow their favorite performers on the screen or the field "religiously." We say they are "fanatics." Every form of play has its pantheon of "immortals." Baseball, Brecht, and the Bible have this single thing in common; they attempt imaginatively to reconstruct a world; they lubricate the imagination and force it to play.

PLAY POWER. To play is to yield oneself to a kind of magic, to enact to oneself the absolute other, to pre-empt the future, to give the lie to the inconvenient world of fact. In play earthly realities become, of a sudden, things of the transient moment, presently left behind, then disposed of and buried in the past: the mind is prepared to accept the unimagined and incredible, to enter a world where different laws apply, to be relieved of all the weights that bear him down, to be free, kingly, unfettered, and divine. . . .—HUGO RAHNER, Man at Play

---

Theater is one of the few ceremonies in modern life whose structure and artfulness sustain the child's-play impulse into adulthood, reviving the primal yearnings for psychic omnipotence. Theater is a testing, an exploration, a reiteration. Where the child wants to touch and to toy with objects to know them and learn, theater allows us to see objects as vessels containing hidden ideas. The playwright re-creates the world and makes the audience play according to his rules; but the viewer makes the connections and his presence wills the performance into being. In theater, as in all authentic play, he retains a sense of power. He is needed in the game; and it cannot be played without him. His response, to a large extent, controls the event.

Play is a rehearsal of the unknown as well as the

familiar; a discovery as well as a confirmation. We say a playwright has a "point of view." The spectator must not only uncover that angle; but his whole experience of re-creation comes from that perspective. Like primitive rituals dramatizing the origins of the cosmos, theater creates a world whose vision can become exemplary. Images can transform consciousness and so renew life. Where the primitive performances are a crucial communal means of remembering the past and bringing the spirit world alive, modern man is always surprised when theater has any visceral effect on life. Our community is so large and cumbersome, so complicated by knowledge and technology, so often dedicated to escape—that rarely is theater seen to have a direct, visible effect on the society. But there are exceptions. Yeats's *Cathleen Ni Houlihan* was a heroic play that sparked participation in the Easter Rising of 1916 in Dublin. "The first night of Beaumarchais' *Marriage of Figaro*," writes Conor Cruise O'Brien "was an episode—a real episode—in the French Revolution, and the dialogue of Bazarov in Turgenev's *Fathers and Sons* set the tone for more than one generation of Russian proto-revolutionists. The plebeians are always in some sense rehearsing the uprising."

Although what has become "sacred" in most modern theater is "commerce," the stage images can still speak directly to man's deepest yearnings and fears; the result can be cathartic. The riots in Dublin after the Abbey Theatre performed J. M. Synge's *The Playboy of the Western World* or the bedlam that broke out the first night of Alfred Jarry's *Ubu Roi* illustrates how the prophecy of a play can penetrate an audience's subconscious life and force a society into a recognition of its real condition.

YEATS AT UBU OPENING. I go to the first performance at Jarry's Ubu Roi, at the Théâtre de l'Oeuvre, with Rhymer. . . . The audience shake their fists at one another, and Rhymer whispers to me, "There are often duels after these performances," and explains to me what is happening on stage. The players are supposed to be dolls, toys, marionettes, and now they are all hopping like wooden frogs, and I can see for myself that the chief personage, who is some kind of king, carries for a sceptre a brush of the kind we use to clean the closet [toilet]. Feeling bound to support the most spirited party, we have shouted for the play, but that night at the Hotel Corneille I am very sad,

for comedy, objectivity, has displayed its growing power once more. I say, After S. Mallarmé, after Verlaine, after G. Moreau, after Puvis de Chavannes, after our own verse, after the faint mixed tints of [Charles] Conder, what more is possible? After us the Savage God.—Autobiography

Children play "rough"; when stage play is good, it is often as dangerous, and always as tense. We say it is "challenging"; we have "wrestled" with ideas. There is no thrill to any performance unless it is "played for keeps." Playing is contest; and our exhilaration comes from living through an imaginative life/death struggle. Ideas can threaten our sense of the world's stability. When images *up-set* the imagination, we often experience the *extraordinary*. At the theater, we want "to be taken by surprise"; in other words, we want to be *seized*. This implies all the ingredients of child's play: awe, fear, struggle. We experience an imaginative history to understand our own; we debate how we would act; we marvel at the body, voice, and word being taken to extremes. We are made more *self*-aware. Through re-creation of the play impulse, we grow.

Technological warfare changes the nature and scope of the ghoulish destruction behind the war game. In Vietnam, for instance, where American firepower dominates the North Vietnamese 1,000 to 1, the drama of the "body count" is still tallied as if it were hand-to-hand combat. "Search-and-destroy" missions are a deadly version of "hide and seek." The aesthetic forms of play have been refined; but they still exist. The rules of battle are clearly set out (the Hague Convention, the Geneva Convention). The fiction of the "fair fight" still carries—in its assump-

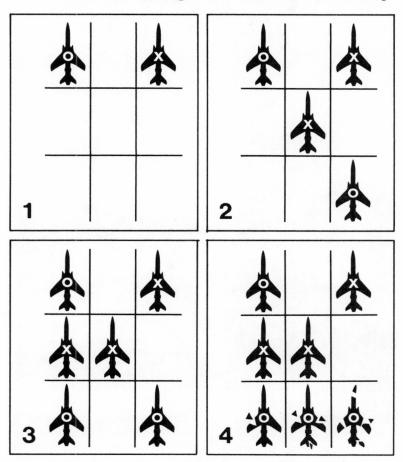

tions—the idea of battle as play that must stick to defined boundaries. Our shock at the atrocities of battle (My Lai, concentration camps) is based on the "unfairness" of the killing. As with theatrical re-creations, war turns values on their head: morality—at least during the time of "playing," "war-time"—is suspended. Ordinary law does not apply. The military fights, and judges itself by its own rules. Machinery (weaponry) takes precedent over man. Man, in turn, is transformed into a fighting "machine." Death to the "enemy" becomes the "good"; life the "bad." Since it is necessary for both the performer and the audience to believe the heroic fantasy being acted out in battle, the military promotes the illusion that the rules of battle are kept. The soldier knows that in battle "anything goes."

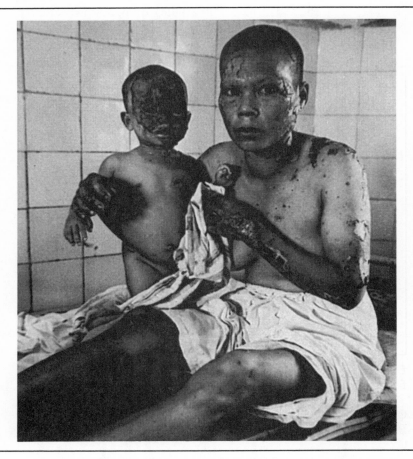

Modern warfare re-creates the drama of technology's unlimited power and invention. At home, technology is touted as a liberation of man from conventional tasks. It is a tool of progress; but when it cannot create a just, benevolent, and abundant society, when its productivity is

frustrated by lack of markets, then the spectacle of its full force against the "enemy" shows off its "goodness."

"War is only a continuation of State policy," wrote Clausewitz, one of the major philosophers of war. Walter Benjamin's statement—"All efforts to render politics aesthetic culminate in one thing—war"—links war to theater.

Not all play is instructive; nor is all theater. Some theater is created merely as a pastime. This is a valid function of playing; and, although it can be as revealing about a child's personality as it is of an audience, it is not as rewarding or life-giving as play where ideas, emotions, and personality are at stake. Inauthentic theater (sports, circus, musical extravaganza, situation comedy) is a distraction; it wants the spectator to forget. This act of re-creation is not *demanding*. We are not truly tested or do we test the world.

The illusion of this kind of theater is that *we are not even in the theater*. Authentic theater structures re-creation for discovery and wants the spectator to *feel* so he can remember and understand. Even Brecht, who argued for an epic theater of distance not involvement, of thought not easy sentiment, was still creating an abrasive, strange world emphasizing a renewed playfulness from the spectator.

The dramatic theatre's spectator says: Yes, I have felt like that too— Just like me— It's only natural— It'll never change— The sufferings of this man appal me, because they are inescapable— That's great art; it all seems the most obvious thing in the world— I weep when they weep, I laugh when they laugh.

*The epic theatre's spectator says: I'd never have
thought it— That's not the way— That's extraordinary,
hardly believable— It's got to stop— The sufferings of
this man appal me, because they are unnecessary— That's
great art; nothing obvious in it— I laugh when they
weep, I weep when they laugh.—BERTOLD BRECHT,
Quoted in Brecht on Theater edited by John Willet*

All play makes its own inclusive universe: baseball,
football, cops-and-robbers. Theater also re-creates a universe, but with a difference. The event is meant to touch our
emotional-historical past in the present, reinterpreting the
world to clarify our real needs and remind us of a primal
connection to *homo sapiens* which other pastimes do not.

*We recall the past not only by recording it but reliving it,
by making present again its fears and delectations. We
anticipate the future not only by preparing for it but by
conjuring up and creating it. Our links to yesterday and
tomorrow depend also on the aesthetic, emotional, and
symbolic aspects of human life—on saga, play, and celebra-
tion. Without festivity and fantasy man would not
really be a historical being at all.—HARVEY COX, The
Feast of Fools*

While society is filled with moments of ritual significance—the ceremonies of birth, death, adulthood ("confirmation," "bar-mitzvah"), technology has desacralized
modern experience. Man sees in himself the power that
for earlier civilizations lay with the gods. Yet, the need
to play is built into man's psychic mechanism: a means of
putting order into one's life and the world, and adjusting
to it. Theater serves this function. "To express his deepest
feelings to himself, man needs a ritual, just as he needs a
language to talk to himself. Ritual does for movement what
language does for sound, transforms it from the inchoate
into the expressive" (Harvey Cox, *The Feast of Fools*).
Theatrical ritual is symbolic action sanctioned by the community. These formal presentations contain and communicate cultural myths which deepen the sense of community by making an audience aware of a shared history.
LeRoi Jones's *Slaveship* traces the Black man from the
galleys of the slave ships that brought him to a white world
through the many roles he has been forced to play in white
society. Arthur Kopit's *Indians* juxtaposes the white man's
view of the Indians with the Indian's sense of the erosion
of his land and his history. The Living Theatre's *Paradise
Now* is a four-hour spectacle, dramatizing levels of consciousness, asking spectators to join the performance,
passing them through special initiation rites. The Open
Theatre's *Serpent* reinvents Genesis to explore the nature of
our modern guilt. These contemporary plays differ in style

and content, but they are all ritualistic initiations into social mythology. They make an audience face its past and work through it imaginatively to an understanding of the possibilities for its future. This is in keeping with the spiritual function of playing—the impulse to overcome time. As Mircea Eliade writes:

*The initiation myths and rites . . . reveal the following fact: the "return to the origin" prepares a new birth, but the new birth is not a repetition of the first physical birth. There is, properly speaking a mystical rebirth, spiritual in nature—in other words, access to a new mode of existence (involving sexual maturity, participation in the sacred and in culture; in short, becoming "open" to Spirit). The basic idea is that, to attain a higher mode of existence, gestation and birth must be repeated; but they are repeated ritually, symbolically. In other words, we here have acts oriented toward the values of Spirit, not behavior from the realm of psycho-physiological activity.
—Myth and Reality*

The yearning behind the theater's re-creations was built into its architecture in earlier times. The sculpture of the Gothic cathedral (the beginning of medieval drama); the sun, moon, and stars painted on the inside of the stage roof of Elizabethan playhouses—presented the spectator not only with a world view, but the *world*: stimulating memory, symbolically showing man the evolution of his "position in the universe."

SHAKESPEARE'S HENRY V

Can this cockpit hold
The vasty fields of France? Or may we cram
Within this wooden O the very casques
That did a fright the air at Agincourt? . . .
Think, when we talk of horses, that you see them
Printing their proud hoofs i' the receiving earth;
For 'tis your thought that now must deck our kings,
Carry them here and there; jumping o'er times,
Turning the accomplishment of many years
Into an hour-glass. . . .

Not only is Shakespeare's theater a circle like the world but he intends the audience to make a universe, condense history, and feel it to be real. A sacred space has been created; and within it, the spirit is capable of confirming everything. This ritual process in which the structure symbolically re-creates the cosmos is as visible in Greek drama as Gothic architecture. At the great Greek festivals, in seats that placed man dramatically between sky and the "center of the universe," Greek history and Greek gods were re-experienced. Here, the community was bound together in a space dedicated to the spirit and metaphorically linking heaven to earth. In the small arena, dwarfed sometimes by as many as 17,000 seats, were reactualizations of the mythic figures who guided them.

THE CITY DIONYSIA: DRAMATIC FESTIVAL AS COSMOS. The importance of the festival was derived not only from the performances of dramatic and lyric poetry but from the fact that it was open to the whole Hellenic world and was an effective advertisement of the wealth and power and public spirit of Athens, no less than the artistic and literary leadership of her sons. . . . Before the performance of the tragedies began, the orphaned of those who had fallen in battle for Athens, such as had reached a suitable age, were caused to parade in the theatre in full armour and receive the blessing of the People. . . . The festival was also made the occasion for the proclamation of honours conferred upon citizens or strangers for conspicuous service to Athens; and it was a natural time for the visits of ambassadors from other states for business requiring publicity. The festival was a time of holiday; prisoners were released on bail to attend the festival. . . .

As a preliminary rite to the festival, though considered not perhaps part of the festival itself, there was a re-enactment of the original advent of Dionysus from Eleutheria. . . .—SIR ARTHUR PICK-ARD-CAMBRIDGE, The Dramatic Festivals of Athens

---

Our conventional modern stage architecture—with its safe proscenium distance, isolated seats, fierce commercialism—reflects the limitations of modern life: deprived of the sacred by technique, boxed into static positions, and literal imaginative responses.

In theater, the individual enters into a clearly defined community. He is connected to the group; and the spectator's response is influenced by those around him. The community helps him to experience the event and himself. Individuality develops not by isolation; but (as the roots of the word imply) by interrelation. Re-creation not only keeps alive the best of man's playful instincts; but the movement from darkness to light is a ritual reworking of rebirth. The audience "awakens" to a world of pristine wonder and mythic size, the spectator's imagination transcends the "profane" existence of everyday cloaked in darkness, reaching out to the unique, mythic world sustained in white light.

Most societies sanction stage re-creations as an acceptable way of coping with the community's festival spirit. Theater can "run riot"; the stage can turn the world upside down to see how it works. In the "confines" of the theater, these activities are isolated and comparatively safe. The re-creations satisfy deep needs in a public. The stage may channel the festival, playful spirit to its highest aesthetic and educational ends: an act of public contemplation. But it is not the only exhibition of "theatrical" re-creation. The fiesta, the Saint's Day, the carnival are all celebrations which reveal the same significant dynamic of stage play. In America, the Mardi Gras, Halloween (only proper for children), and a few paltry football "celebrations" are vestiges of this anarchic spirit. We are a culture whose goals and games stress work, discipline, and practicality. Other societies (often those where oppression is most visible, where class differences are the most rigid) still carry on the tradition. Then, festival is a stop-time. New roles are invented; conventional ones are abandoned. The "spoilsport," the "kill-joy" are banished. New "Kings" and "Queens" are elected and installed along with their "court," just as Sir Toby Belch or Sir John Falstaff were merry stage prototypes for the drunken Lords of Misrule who presided over Elizabethan May games.

FROM A PURITAN DIARY. They have also certain papers, wherein is painted some bablery or other of imagery work, and these they call "my Lord of Misrule's badges." These they give to everyone that will give money for them to maintain them in their heathenry, devilry, whoredom, drunkenness, pride and what not. And who will not be buxom to them and give them money for their devilish cognizances, they are mocked and flouted not a little. And so assotted are some that they will not only give them money to maintain their abomination withal, but also wear their badges and cognizances in their hats or caps openly. . . .—C. L. BARBER, Shakespeare's Festive Comedy

In the theater, the mind "lets itself go"; there, it is free to discover and to accept in an environment liberated from the everyday. Public festivals—from the Elizabethan May game to the modern fiesta—destroyed social boundaries and allowed the public to experiment with new roles. The bacchanalia was purgative: mixing the play spirit's impulse for joy with a release from the weight of sadness and terror in daily life. Each festival, like the theater, expresses the obsessions, dreams, and character unique to its society. Theater makes this symbolic action in the imagination; the public festival makes each person's *action* symbolic. Costumes, masks, role-reversals, flouting of authority—all aspects of stage theatricality—are incorporated into life-play. Octavio Paz describes the meaning behind fiestas, the energy and passion for playfulness which clarifies the life that theatre isolates and makes into art.

PLAY-TIME. The fiesta's function, then, is more utilitarian than we think: waste attracts or promotes wealth, and is an investment like any other, except that the returns on it cannot be measured or counted. What is sought is potency, life, health. In this sense the fiesta like the gift and the offering is one of the most ancient of economic forms.

This interpretation has always seemed to me to be incomplete. The fiesta is by nature sacred, literally and figuratively, and above all it is the advent of the unusual. It is governed by its own special rules, that set it apart from other days, and it has a logic, an ethic and even an economy that

are often in conflict with everyday norms. It all occurs in an enchanted world: time is transformed to a mythical past or a total present: space, the scene of the fiesta, is turned into a gaily decorated world of its own; and the persons taking part cast off all human or social rank and become, for the moment, living images. And everything takes place as if it were not so, as if it were a dream. But whatever happens, our actions have a greater lightness, a different gravity. . . .

In certain fiestas the very notion of order disappears. Chaos comes back and license rules. Anything is permitted: the customary hierarchies vanish, along with all social, sex, caste and trade distinctions. Men disguise themselves as women, gentlemen as slaves, the poor as the rich. The army, the clergy, the law are ridiculed. Obligatory sacrilege, ritual profanation is committed. Love becomes promiscuity. Sometimes the fiesta becomes a Black Mass. Regulations, habits and customs are violated. Respectable people put away dignified expressions and conservative clothes that isolate them, dress up in gaudy colors, hide behind a mask and escape from themselves.

. . . By means of the fiesta, society frees itself from the norms it has established. It ridicules its gods, its principles, and its laws; it denies its own self.

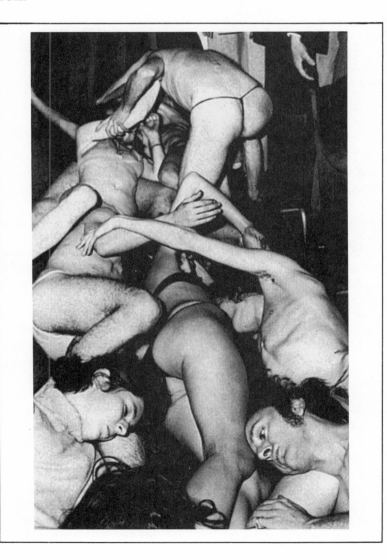

The fiesta is a revolution in the most literal sense of the word. In the confusion that it generates, society is dissolved, is drowned in so far as it is an

organism ruled according to certain laws and principles. But it drowns in itself, in its own original chaos and liberty. Everything is united: good and evil, day and night, the sacred and the profane. Everything merges, loses shape and individuality and returns to the primordial mass. The fiesta is a cosmic experiment, an experiment in disorder, re-uniting contradictory elements and principles in order to bring about a renascence of life. Ritual death promotes rebirth, vomiting increases the appetite; the orgy, sterile in itself, renews the fertility of the mother or of the earth. The fiesta is a return to a remote and undifferentiated stage prenatal and presocial. It is a return that is also a beginning. . . .

The group emerges purified and strengthened from this plunge into chaos. It has immersed itself in its own origins, in the womb from which it came. . . .—OCTAVIO PAZ, The Labyrinth of Solitude

Boundaries are crucial to the tension of stage or public re-creation. Real or imaginary, they are the walls which surround us: giving safety and shape to experience on the one hand, abrasion and pressure on the other. We cross

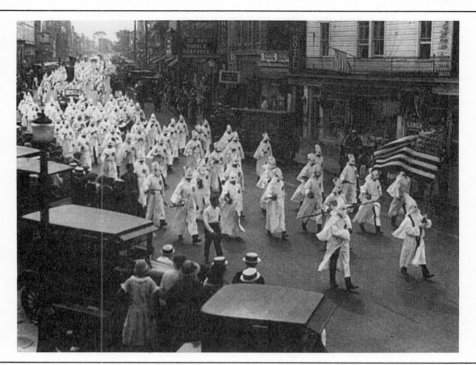

boundaries at our own risk: there is a threat of loss in the action, but *also* the hope of gain. Boundaries, then, can also be a source of exhilaration and danger. The excitement and sense of purpose in breaking down boundaries—as the fiesta or the experimental play illustrates—comes from the fact that it *exists*. In conventional theater, action is bounded by time and space. Playwrights like Luigi Pirandello and Harold Pinter use the proscenium "boundary line" and the expectations of re-creations within these limits to extend theater beyond them. In *The Dwarfs*, Pinter discusses the fluctuation of boundaries, the continual revision of limits which his later plays dramatize unspoken:

The rooms we live in . . . open and shut. . . . Can't you see?
They change shape at their own will. I couldn't grumble
if only they would keep some consistency. But they don't.
And I can't tell the limits, the boundaries which I've been
lead to believe are natural.

With guerrilla theater or happenings, the event redefines its theatrical limits. This is also true of public celebrations: actions may occur over a number of days and places. Each re-creation has its own historical/social context, but all are testing the ultimate boundary of life/death. Theater incarnates the fact of boundaries and the process by which man tries to reinvent and stabilize them through play.

Just as the playwright seeks to re-create his vision of the world through stage action, a nation often reinvents an idea of its heroic stature and mythic destiny through war. "War and everything to do with it remains fast in the daemonic and magical bonds of play," writes Johann Huizinga in *Homo Ludens*.

LIONEL TIGER ON GENERALS IN DRAG. . . . Males are very fragile; they can only operate in very fantasy structures—like the Pentagon, like the U.S. Government—with seals and all the wings and eagles. They have this fantastic panoply that males create. Males are always in drag, in a sense, even if they're in the Pentagon, always constantly elaborating these highly mythical structures.— Time Magazine

---

These re-creations are dangerous; but they are still played compulsively. We know that war leads to death, and civilizations can be completely changed in the struggle. But the impulse behind it is the contest; and the play is carried out with a sense of sacred dedication. In war, battle is elevated to mythic struggle: whatever is being contested is subjugated to a higher symbolic struggle. The duel pits one nation's honor, glory, and history against another's, war, rehearsed as "war games," fought in "combat theaters," revives and sustains an imaginary destiny. Like theatrical re-creations, it is a way of remembering the past and sustaining the ideal of a future. "One wages war in order to obtain a decision of holy validity," writes Huizinga. "The test of the will of the gods is victory or defeat." Political goals are never as certain or profoundly significant as the even deeper need to win. What is at stake is the whole body and soul of a society.

韓國人跟着鐵路向前
中國人跟着左边路
한국인은 철길을따라앞으로가고
중국인은 왼편 길을따라가시오
KOREANS STRAIGHT AHEAD
FOLLOW RAILROAD TRACKS
CHINESE FOLLOW ROAD
ON LEFT

RICHARD NIXON UPON INVADING CAMBODIA: "OPERATION TOTAL VICTORY." Small nations all over the world will find themselves under attack from within and from without. If when the chips are down the world's most powerful nation—the United States of America—acts like a pitiful, helpless giant, the forces of totalitarianism and anarchy will threaten free nations and free institutions throughout the world.

It is not our power but our will and character that is being tested tonight. . . .

The question all Americans must ask and answer tonight is this:

Does the richest and strongest nation in the history of the world have the character to meet direct threats by a group which rejects all efforts to win a just peace, ignores our warning, tramples on solemn agreements, violates the neutrality and uses our prisoners as hostages? . . . I promised to win a just peace. I shall keep that promise.

The ritual nature of combat was clearer in earlier centuries. The drummer boys, the marching songs, the advancing front lines with both camps facing one another on an open field—emphasized the play behind war's "deadly seriousness." The time for the battle was set; the rules defined. "Tactics" and "strategy" were a more visible "game plan"—a staged, spectacular re-creation of heroism. In the medieval disputes between Italian principalities, for instance, the *condottieri* (mercenaries) fought battles noted for their playfulness. The military historian Charles Oman wrote:

The consequences of leaving the conduct of the war in the hands of great mercenary captains was that it came to be waged as a mere tactical exercise or a game of chess, the aim being to maneuver the enemy into an impossible position, and then capture him, rather than exhaust him by a series of costly battles. It was suspected that the condottieri, like dishonest pugilists, sometimes settled beforehand that they would draw the game. Battles when they did occur were often very bloodless affairs. . . . Machiavelli cites cases and general actions in which there were only two or three men-at-arms slain, though the prisoners numbered by the hundreds.

Technology, the symbolic extension of man and his physical potential, is tested. "Technology is materialized fantasy," Philip Slater has written in *The Pursuit of Loneliness.* "We are ruled today by the material manifestations of fantasies of previous generations." War, like child's play, is a re-creation which dramatizes the dream of omnipotence. America's *saturation bombing* of Vietnam, the mythic names for its missile systems—"Nike-Zeus," "Skybolt"—are indications of the fantasizing behind technology. American planes are named in imitation of fierce Indian tribes (Mohawk, Choctaw), magical figures of mythic strength (The Jolly Green Giant, Hercules, Dragon Ship, Voodoo), heroic hunters (Sea Knight, Skyhawk, Tiger, Crusader, Vigilante, Intruder). Unable to fulfill the primal role of hunter, man wills technology to kill with a precision and in numbers unheard of in his history. We may be horrified by the effects of war, but the society is also clearly obsessed with the beauty of technology's performance. The "miracle weapons"—the new bombs, the special guns, the planes—perform "magical" feats: towns are eliminated by pressing a button; M-16s fire twenty rounds a second, accurate up to five hundred yards; missiles can be controlled by computers—there is no end to the intricacy of technological innovation. In Vietnam, the "overkill' (between 1965–1969, 4,580,000 tons of explosives—six and a half times the amount detonated in Korea—were dropped in Vietnam by U.S. forces) is an indication of the society's psychic impotence and yearning for a "heroic" future. Afraid of its spiritual demise, America kills as proof that it is alive. There is also a symmetrical delight to the performances.

ACTION PAINTING. B52 bombers, flying from Guam over 2,500 miles away from Thailand, dropping bombs from 40,000 feet so that they cannot be seen or heard from below, can wipe out an entire valley. In one of these "saturation" or "carpet" raids, fifty square miles of jungle can suddenly explode into flame without warning from a rain of fire bombs. These raids are frequent, and in the areas they strike, nothing will live, animal or human, friend or enemy. It is almost as effective on plants and animals as defoliation, which kills three hundred acres in 4 minutes. . . .—PHILIP SLATER, Pursuit of Loneliness

---

On stage, man re-creates himself in his own dimension, re-experiencing problems which beset him. The spectator is symbolically involved but set apart. Distance of some kind is necessary for appreciation: both for the actor, who *needs* to be near the audience, and for the audience, who must feel some relation to the actor. In war, technology—(designed by man to give him superhuman power)—acts out

its demonic possibilities—the destruction of human life. The position from which we view the "accomplishment" parallels that of a theatrical spectator. In our modern technological warfare, much of the killing is done at a great distance from the enemy. The soldier (actor) and the public *feel* powerful *and* human because they are so physically apart from the actuality of their actions. Killing is at a safe distance, preserving our psychic life. The aesthetic pleasure of technology's range and magnified power demands this distance. The delight of one American in killing a peasant epitomizes the paradox: "I ran the little mother all over the place hosing him with guns but somehow or other we just didn't hit him. Finally, he turned on us and stood there facing us with a rifle. We really busted his ass then. Blew him up like a toy balloon." War acts out ideas contained in the scenario of State policy along with the society's subconscious wishes. For governments to make policy acceptable, war must be turned into an aesthetic experience. This, in a technological society, is the function of propaganda. In earlier parades, maneuvers, flamboyant drills, and costumes were intentional, spectacular public glorifications of its warriors. Their movements and costumes, the nature of their service separated them from the ordinary world. They were dream figures.

Now, the media has turned war almost totally into an aesthetic experience. We watch the victories (rarely the defeats) through the same communication channels that provide our daily entertainment. The maneuvers, machinery, maps, and men are always visible, but at a safe distance.

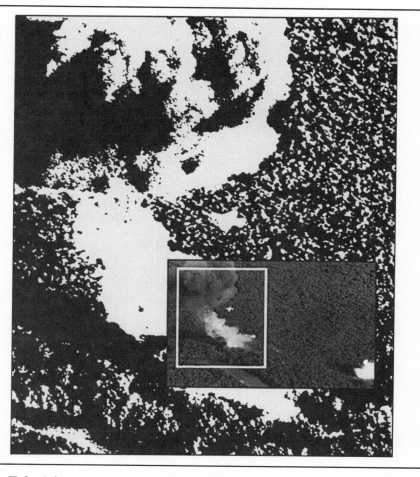

Television is everyman's proscenium arch. Technology makes the spectacle of war exciting and overwhelms the public with a sense of prophecy.

Like theater, battle exaggerates emotion and events. Human action takes on surreal proportions. Suspicious of technology yet longing for miracles, American society turns it to triumph in battle. War films, war novels, war reportage, even war colleges and training camps transform battle into art. The impulse was foreshadowed by the rationalizations of Italian Futurist Emilio Marinetti who justified the Fascist invasion of Ethiopia on artistic grounds!

FUTURIST MANIFESTO.

. . . For twenty-seven years we Futurists have rebelled against the branding of war as anti-aesthetic. . . . Accordingly we state:

War is beautiful because it establishes man's dominion over the subjugated machinery by means of gas masks, terrifying megaphones, flame throwers and small tanks.

War is beautiful because it initiates the metalization of the human body.

War is beautiful because it enriches a flowering meadow with the fiery orchids of machine guns. War is beautiful because it combines gunfire, the cannonades, the ceasefire, the scents and stench of putrefaction into a symphony.

War is beautiful because it creates new architecture, like that of the big tanks, the geometrical formation flights, the smoke spirals from burning villages, and many others.

Poets and artists of Futurism . . . remember these principles of an aesthetic of war so that your struggle for a new literature and a new graphic art . . . may be illumined by them.

War is the ultimate extension of the play impulse to re-create the world in one's own image, to start afresh by eliminating the sources of abrasion. In play, victories may be tangible symbolic conquests; but they stop short of actual destruction. On stage and in life, play is a mechanism which reroutes aggressive instincts and channels them into more socially acceptable and benign forms. The form itself is important and changes as the society changes. Each person who plays, whether he makes a piece of theater or participates in sport, is living out rules, attitudes, and patterns absorbed from his culture. The form of recreation, its literal pattern, tells us about the assumptions of the society. Baseball became America's national pastime in the early decades of the twentieth century's incredible industrialization. The shock and abrasion of this growth, as well as its pleasures, were partially reflected in their new-found passion for baseball. "Sport is tied to industry," Jacques Ellul has written in *The Technological Society*. "Because it represents a reaction against industrial society." Where industry made time of the essence, in baseball time was expansive: games ambled along at their own leisurely pace. Where industry forced great proportions of the population off the land and into the city, baseball created a pastoral illusion (the stadiums with their great shards of green turf existing amid the stifling slums industrial exploitation had created). At a time of enterprise capitalism, of pluck·'n luck—baseball absorbed all the workaday axioms of capitalism and reinforced them in an elaborate mechanism of fun. Success in baseball rested on the very tenets that brought success in business: efficiency, speed, technique, responsible risk.

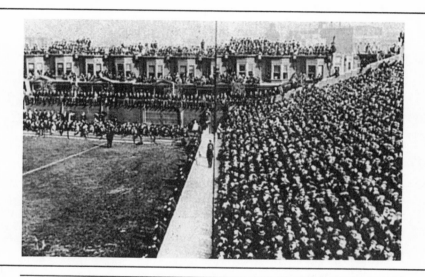

FROM A BASEBALL HANDBOOK. He jeers the officials and indulges in hot arguments with his neighbors, stamping and ranting. . . . All the time his vital organs are summoned into strenuous sympathy and he draws deep breaths of pure air. He may be weary when the game is over but for it he will eat and sleep better, his step will be more determined, his eyes will cease resembling those of a dead fish. . . . He goes back to his desk or bench next day with a smiling face.

Managerial skill was also important to the game. The player had to *produce*, and statistics for every aspect of his performance were as carefully recorded and computed as the gross national product. Alienated and confused by the statistics of industrial society, the baseball spectator could

be a specialist on equal footing with any man in the
stadium. The drama of baseball was the drama of productivity: man's effort distilled happily into numbers—
RBI, ERA, BA, etc. Medieval theater attested to the
Church's accuracy and baseball affirmed a new world of
accounting and double-entry bookkeeping.

The competition between teams is a play-battle of in-
dustries. Spectators "root for their home team," and accept
in play the unacceptable in life. In this staged production,
people are treated as property. In baseball, "trading,"
"bonuses," "fines" are a means of improving efficiency and
sharpening competition. Within this often brutal allegiance
of players and management, when a "performer" becomes
a "star," his appeal dramatizes another aspect of American society's dream. With innate skill, often without education (but with a few good breaks)—a performer through
baseball can have "all the good things in life": money,

recognition, mobility. Baseball re-creates all of the industrial society's central assumptions.

The rules of the game are learned from childhood. In order to play, they must be strictly followed. In the staging of the game, the umpire assumes absolute authority. Spectators and players might argue with him; but, in his black suit—symbolically set off from the colorful players—he is the official, formal word of law. He maintains the boundaries. Violation and disruption of the game means banishment from its play universe. Acquiescence to authority is dramatized as the only means of surviving conflict. Also, since statistics in baseball become history and are crucial to the fantasy drama the game inspires, to change the rules would mean that the hitting and pitching averages would have no relationship to the past. This, for fans, is intolerable. If the world is changing daily, if the history of their country is murky and unrecollected, the history of baseball, at least, should be clear, accessible, and verifiable. This need, which baseball fulfills in play, society denies in life.

Baseball is a spectacle: on the field, its drama is staged. The background against which it is played is just as much a self-conscious environment as a theater, containing assumptions about man's function and the attitude of a society toward his position in space. In baseball's staging, the player is part of a team, but he controls his own territory. The circumference of his playing space is usually respected by others; on the field, his territorial rights are very clearly observed. He has "elbow room." Baseball, as opposed to football, focuses and isolates the individual effort. We watch one thing at a time.

Football re-creates a ritual war which is a spectacle of technique. The players are instruments of punishment and attack. Their training mechanizes action: performance must be superhuman and precise. Speaking of this specialization, Jerry Kramer discussed the intention behind the training of the late Vince Lombardi:

He makes us execute the same plays over and over, a hundred times, two hundred times, until we do every little thing right automatically. He works to make the kickoff return team perfect. He ignores nothing. Technique, technique, technique, over and over and over, until we feel like we're going crazy. But we win.

Man becomes an engine; and he re-creates an ideal setting for this new engineering. The battle is bolstered by medicine and new technology (uniforms, special helmets, etc.). Science is also at play on the football field. The strategy, the "scouts," the films of the "enemy's tactics" transform the game into a pseudoscience whose motive in play (as it is in war) is reflected in its vernacular of success "to kill," "slaughter," "annihilate," "multilate" the opponent. The

dream of victory is shared by the spectators who are often totally carried away by the spectacle of action and the assumptions they imply. The message implicit in this spectacle is—violence pays.

One style of playing influences and overlaps with others, just as the remnants of the Elizabethan stage affected Restoration theater although the society had drastically changed. The looseness of baseball's grouping contrasts with the more modern spectacle of football where men are crammed tightly together, identified only by number, and battle ferociously against the opponent in a spectacle where the fittest survive. If baseball was the recreation of an industrial society, football—and its fantastic following—meets the needs of a technological one. The function is both to distract the spectator from the abrasion of modern life and reinforce social convictions. The body, on the field, is turned into a machine; the spectators become a mass. All energy is directed to the goal of total, overwhelming victory. (Red China, which has reinstituted Ping-Pong as its national sport, only announces who has played, not who wins.)

Technicized sport was first developed in the United States, the most conformist of all countries, and . . . it was then developed as a matter of course by the dictatorships, Fascist, Nazi, and Communist, to the point that it became an indispensable constituent element of totalitarian regimes.—JACQUES ELLUL, The Technological Society

NEW YORK JET END GEORGE SAUER ON FOOT-
BALL'S WAR. There is unqualified effort to overcome and rise above other men, and to be Number
One is the ultimate objective. As the fittest are in
the process of surviving, almost any means may be
employed for their aggrandizement. . . .

One of the most admired traits in football is ag-
gressiveness toward the opponent. . . . One manda-
tory quality for football players is to withstand intimidation. Rules are by no means inviolable, and
intentional transgressions are deemed integral to
the pursuance of the end: the survival of the fittest. . . . The opponent is judged by the superficial
criterion of uniform color. This serves to determine
the ethicality—or its absence—of the opponent's

particular actions, and what may be condemned in
him may be justified in oneself. To attempt to generate hate for an opponent is considered conducive
to the realizing of the end of establishing superi-
ority. . . . It seems that physical degradation is an
ingrained feature of football.

Where a technological society fragments work and limits
function, football re-creates a world where these elements
are placed in a heroic framework and their destructive
values are spiritually justified. Strangled by the pace of the
culture and suffocated in their own technological isolation—

the spectator, through the game, senses a new community and clear mission. Football's fantasy creates—as does all play—a symbolic transcendence of conventional Time. Football takes this to the extreme: exaggerating and manipulating Time as a crucial part of its drama, turning Time's oppressive weight in a technological existence to excitement in play. The performers on the field control Time: the clock no longer rules the production line, but liberates the playground. Different laws apply. Players, we say, "eat up the clock," "kill the clock," "let the clock run out."

In all types of ritual re-creation, man's psychic need to start again dominates the event. The implication is that theater on stage or in life can change us. It can. Many re-creations can satisfy destructive impulses. To understand the process of play behind them is to be protected and aware of the unfulfilled life they mirror in their dream world of rules, boundaries, costumes, and codes of behavior. One of the barometers of a culture's health is its ceremonies. Do

they put man in deeper touch with his society and himself? America's pathological historical memory can be linked to its lack of authentic, pervasive ceremonies. Baseball and football make a new history, but not a real one; war recalls the war dead, but not the complex reasons for fighting.

Most of our re-creations are merely recreations. They do not redefine us or extend our understanding of experience.

This is where stage play attains its dignity and importance. It distills and comments on the life-shows around it. Theater is not simply dealing with diversion, but with truth; not simply entertainment, but ethics. It expands consciousness. This process is a life force, and a tool for survival. Shakespeare absorbed the patterns of Elizabethan festival and found in them both the seeds of structure and content for many of his plays (*Twelfth Night, As You Like It, A Midsumm'er-Night's Dream*). Familiar spectacles are turned to an imaginative testing of boundaries and the function of festival in society. As Prince Hal says to Falstaff, the archetypal Lord of Misrule, "If all the year were playing holidays/To sport would be as tedious as work;/But when they seldom come, they wished for come. . . ." Playwrights from every century and society strive for this same compression. Wycherly outlines the hypocrisy in the Restoration show of manners; Brecht distills the patterns of history in his spectacles of war and politics; Beckett goes still deeper to show us the spiritual yearning behind our gaming instinct.

The playwright, the director, and the actor are engaged in ways of celebrating and revealing the living moment, re-creating the world to make an audience see and feel ideas in a new way. Plays are memory banks and culture probes. By observing the specifics of their mimetic craft, we—the spectators—can refine our relationship to the profound and dramatic interrelation of man with man, object, space, and society. The stage is the most ruthless, gorgeous exhibition of the dynamic of play that rules not only art, but every day.

ILLUS-TRATIONS